TWELVE
YEARS *of*
TURBULENCE

TWELVE YEARS *of* TURBULENCE

The Inside Story of
American Airlines' Battle for Survival

GARY KENNEDY
with
Terry Maxon

FOREWORD BY ROGER STAUBACH

A SAVIO REPUBLIC BOOK
An Imprint of Post Hill Press

TWELVE YEARS OF TURBULENCE
The Inside Story of American Airlines' Battle for Survival
© 2018 by Gary Kennedy and Terry Maxon
All Rights Reserved

ISBN: 978-1-68261-488-4
ISBN (eBook): 978-1-68261-489-1

Cover Design by Tricia Principe, principedesign.com
Interior Design and Composition by Greg Johnson/Textbook Perfect

posthillpress.com
New York • Nashville
Published in the United States of America

To my father, who proved that hard work, a sense of humor, and a good day fishing are the marks of a life well-lived.

GARY KENNEDY

To my wife, Jannett, and children, Lindsey and Stephen, who endured too many days and years wondering when I was going to finish my story and come home.

TERRY MAXON

CONTENTS

FOREWORD

By Roger Staubach

In late 2000, my friend Charlie Pistor, a member of the American Airlines board of directors, called and asked if I would consider joining the board. Charlie explained that he was retiring from the board and thought I would be an excellent replacement. I told Charlie that I was interested, but would have to give it some thought.

At the time, I was chairman and CEO of The Staubach Company, a commercial real estate business I cofounded in 1977. The Staubach Company was growing rapidly in Texas and expanding into a number of major metropolitan areas across the country. Even though I was incredibly busy, this was a great opportunity with a company that I've always admired.

Over the years, I watched American Airlines grow into the world's largest airline and contribute immensely to the economic success of North Texas. As a graduate of the Naval Academy and former member of the armed services, I have a particular admiration for the pilots of American because so many of them also started their careers in the military. Even more impressive was the fact that American Airlines had almost one hundred thousand employees worldwide and was one of the largest employers in North Texas. The idea of working with the men and women of

American Airlines—pilots, flight attendants, mechanics, ground personnel, and others—made me proud.

Even more compelling was the fact that my wife, Marianne, and I were longtime residents of North Texas. We moved to Dallas in 1969 when I joined the Dallas Cowboys, and we've never lived anywhere else. I've been married for over fifty years and learned early on that it works out best if I consult with Marianne before taking on a new business opportunity. As we talked about the prospect of joining the American board, we agreed that it sounded too good to pass up. Several days later, I had lunch with Don Carty, who was then CEO of American. By the time we finished lunch, I told Don that I would be honored to become a member of the board.

I officially joined the board of directors of American Airlines and its parent, AMR Corporation, in July 2001. I was eager to contribute to the success of the company.

After completing my professional football career, I've followed the same routine almost every morning. When I wake up, I turn on the TV as I run on the treadmill or lift weights before heading into the office. On the morning of September 11, 2001, (just two months after joining the American board), I was in the middle of a workout when I heard the news anchor announce that a plane had crashed into the World Trade Center in New York City. Like the rest of the world, I had no idea of the profound events that were unfolding.

When I arrived at the office, I learned that an emergency meeting of the American board had been scheduled for later that morning. Along with my fellow board members, I listened as CEO Don Carty and chief operating officer Gerard Arpey outlined what they knew about the terrorist strike and what it meant for the future of the airline. I found it difficult to accept that thousands of people had been killed, that two of our aircraft had been destroyed, as well as two United Airlines jets, and that the nation's entire air traffic system had been shut down.

The years that followed 9/11 were difficult for American Airlines. In addition to the tremendous human toll, the company lost billions of dollars and the future looked bleak. I've faced plenty of hardship and difficult challenges during my career, both in the business world and in the world of sports, but those seemed inconsequential compared to the events of 9/11 and what lie ahead for American Airlines.

By March 2003, the company's lawyers were preparing to file for bankruptcy. Just two months earlier, the board approved the appointment of Gary Kennedy as the company's new general counsel. His appointment didn't come as a surprise to me. I had worked with him on several real estate deals that The Staubach Company negotiated for American when he was vice president of American's real estate and construction department. I thought he was the perfect guy to lead the airline's legal affairs, particularly during those difficult days.

I came to rely heavily on Gary's advice and judgment during the many years he served as the company's chief lawyer. Despite the departure of two CEOs, several CFOs, and other senior executives, I was glad that Gary remained a steady presence on the executive team.

As I settled into my role as a board member, I was struck by the sheer volume of difficult issues facing the company. At times, it was overwhelming. The company was under constant attack from competitors, it faced skyrocketing fuel prices and complex labor issues, and its balance sheet was in dire need of repair. For years, the company teetered on the brink of bankruptcy. The board's primary focus was saving American Airlines and returning it to health and prosperity.

But it wasn't easy, and, as board members, we often disagreed about the best way to proceed. Likewise, we didn't always see eye-to-eye with our employees. As we faced one crisis after another, our relationship with labor was tested time and again. Despite the difficulties, I have nothing but the greatest respect for the employees of American Airlines and their dedication to the success of the company. During my days with the Dallas Cowboys, coach Tom Landry was fond of saying, "A true test of character isn't how you are on your best days, but how you act on your worst days." Many of the days during my tenure on the board were clearly some of the worst for American.

As a board member, I felt a deep sense of responsibility to the employees of American and to the North Texas community. Maybe I had a heightened concern for these folks because Dallas is my home; maybe it was because many of these people were my friends and neighbors. As I watched the company struggle, I was keenly aware that livelihoods and families hung in the balance. There were times we were unsure what course to take or if our plans for recovery had any chance of success. Things got so desperate that it felt like we needed to throw a Hail Mary pass in order for American to survive.

The story that unfolds in the pages of this book chronicles the extraordinary events that took place at American Airlines during the years between 2001 and 2013. These are the same years that I served as a director of this great company. *Twelve Years of Turbulence* is a remarkable story. Through it all, I was proud to stand with the extraordinary professionals at American Airlines. Their resilience and strength of character was a true test of the American spirit.

PROLOGUE

It was still dark when the alarm went off in my Manhattan hotel room in the early morning hours of November 29, 2011. But going back to sleep wasn't an option. In less than two hours, events would be set in motion that would have far-reaching consequences for tens of thousands of people, and, for me, test my stamina and resilience in ways I could never imagine.

I left the hotel at approximately 6:15 a.m. It was surprisingly warm for late November as I made the short walk to the law offices of Weil, Gotshal & Manges. I made this trip so many times over the years that I could practically do it blindfolded. It was *déjà vu*. Just eight years earlier, in 2003, I made the same walk, for the same purpose. But unlike the previous occasion, this time I would complete the mission.

It was eerily quiet when I arrived at Weil's office. The first person I saw was Steve Karotkin, a senior partner in the firm's restructuring department. Ordinarily, he would greet me with a caustic barb drawn from his repertoire of irreverent jokes, but not that morning. Everyone was focused on the task at hand.

Shortly before 7 a.m., my associate general counsel, Kathryn Koorenny, and I hovered outside the cubicle of a Weil paralegal. Our eyes were glued to the paralegal's keyboard as she made multiple entries on her computer. A few minutes later, the paralegal turned to us and casually said, "Okay, you're filed."

These simple words understated the profound event that had just occurred—American Airlines, once the world's largest airline, had filed for bankruptcy.

It all happened with the simple stroke of a key while most everyone slept. Only one reporter, Terry Maxon of *The Dallas Morning News*, learned of the filing ahead of time and ran a front-page story in that morning's edition of the paper.

There was no turning back. We had embarked on the final leg of a journey to save American Airlines, a journey that began many years earlier.

CHAPTER 1

SINGLEMINDED

I was seated in my office overlooking the Wasatch Mountains. It was March 1984. My phone rang. On the other end of the line was Jaynne Allison, a close friend from our days in law school at the University of Utah. We both graduated four years earlier and I was working as an associate in a Salt Lake City law firm. As a young lawyer, I was an overachieving, Type A personality with boundless energy, confident that I would soon conquer the world, or at least the legal market in Salt Lake City. Back then, I ate, slept, and lived to practice law. My career was a dream come true.

I hadn't heard much from Jaynne recently so I was excited to speak with her. She left Salt Lake several months earlier to join the legal department of American Airlines. After catching up on friends from law school and our personal lives, Jaynne teased a question that I had never considered, but one that upended the trajectory of my career and my life.

"We have an opening at American for an attorney. You should apply for the job."

"Interesting idea," I said. "But I'm not sure about leaving the mountains of Salt Lake City for the flatlands of Dallas."

"Come on. The airline business is exciting. It's a sexy industry. You'll love it. Besides, Dallas isn't so bad. Think about it and get back to me."

"OK, I'll think about it."

At the time, I had my sights set on making partner at the law firm in record time. The thought of leaving the firm to work for a corporation, much less one in Texas, had never crossed my mind. But Jaynne was right. The airline business is sexy. I was quickly seduced by the allure of traveling all over the world. The more I thought about it, the more I became interested in the idea. I knew Jaynne was a good lawyer, but I had never thought of her as a salesperson. It turns out she was pretty good at both.

A few weeks later, I found myself seated comfortably in first class on an American Airlines Boeing 727 headed to Dallas-Fort Worth for an interview. I walked into the AA headquarters building the next morning and soon felt the energy and pull of the airline business. By the end of the day I was hooked, and three months later I had a new job as a staff attorney in the American Airlines legal department.

From my first day on the job, I set my sight on one goal—I wanted to be general counsel of the airline. Had I not been so green, perhaps I would have tempered that aspiration.

In 1984, Al Casey and Bob Crandall were at the helm of American. Casey was chairman of the board and chief executive officer, and Crandall served as president. Just six years earlier, Congress enacted the Airline Deregulation Act, legislation that fundamentally changed the face of the airline industry. Under the deregulation act, the Civil Aeronautics Board was phased out and no longer controlled things like airfares and the routes flown by carriers. It was a time of upheaval and enormous change.

In an effort to respond to the new post-deregulation environment, American rolled out the "Growth Plan," an effort to expand the airline at breakneck speed as a means to drive down average costs and outpace the competition. The company had just completed one of the largest aircraft deals in aviation history, the purchase of hundreds of McDonnell Douglas aircraft—the MD-80 workhorse, or as we referred to it, the Super 80. The aircraft was lauded as state of the art, with vastly improved fuel efficiency and a

2-by-3 seating configuration that reduced the number of passengers flying in middle seats.

I watched with fascination as the airline experienced the highs and lows of an ultracompetitive industry. I was in awe of the actions we took to crush our competitors and what they would do in kind to us. We added capacity to get a jump on our rivals, and they responded by adding even more capacity on top of ours. We announced a double miles AAdvantage promotion and they answered with a triple mileage promotion for their own frequent flyer program.

It was, as Bob Crandall once remarked, the closest thing you could get to legalized warfare. The business was incredibly exciting, yet chaotic, destined to result in a weak, maimed industry, one lacking earnings sufficient to return satisfactory results to shareholders and often lacking the capacity to invest the billions needed to profitably grow the business.

During those early days, I made a point to arrive early to work and leave late. Crandall was a workaholic, and he expected those around him to keep a similar schedule. Knowing that, I went out of my way to make sure that he knew who I was.

The legal department was located immediately adjacent to the executive offices. Late at night, Crandall often made his presence known by marching through the department like a general ready to inspect the troops. His voice boomed as he bellowed for Dick Lempert, who was then general counsel. As soon as I heard Crandall's voice, I would jump out of my chair and rush into the hallway, hoping for an opportunity to introduce myself. The tactic worked on several occasions, and I often wonder just what Crandall must have thought of the young lawyer lurking in the hallway.

My first several years at American were fast and furious. The job turned out to be everything I hoped for. There were only twelve in-house lawyers in the department so we worked on anything and everything that came in the door. I traveled all over the world—Europe, Asia, Australia, the Middle East—negotiating agreements that powered airline flight reservation systems. I got the chance to sue iconic Pan American World Airways, was co-lead on the acquisition of TWA's European route system, and oversaw a massive set of antitrust lawsuits with travel agents and airlines involving our computer reservation system known as SABRE. The list of great projects was endless.

Then, in 1991, my friend Jaynne Allison once again managed to change the direction of my career. A few years earlier, she left the legal department and was then vice president of the company's real estate and construction department. Jaynne asked me to join her as a managing director and oversee the real estate arm of the department. It would be a big promotion, one step away from a coveted vice-president position.

I had mixed emotions about leaving the active practice of law, particularly given my goal of one day being general counsel. But I quickly accepted, knowing that Crandall wanted executives to be well-rounded and exposed to numerous aspects of the airline business. My stay in real estate and construction extended for a total of twelve years, with the last seven as vice president of the department.

The time I spent in corporate real estate was marked by a huge push to build new airport terminals and facilities at many of our largest airports. After many years handling big legal transactions and directing mega "bet the company" litigation, I found myself wading through new territory. For a guy in his early thirties, I was confident, maybe even a little cocky, about my legal skills. However, construction was a different animal. I could hardly handle a cordless drill, let alone read a set of blueprints, but quickly found myself sporting a hard hat and inspecting construction sites all over the country.

It was trial by fire. I was put in charge of planning and overseeing a new 1.3 billion-dollar terminal at John F. Kennedy International Airport, a billion dollar-plus terminal in Miami (a project that was a financial and managerial nightmare before it was finally completed), and making a deal with Dallas/Fort Worth International Airport to construct an international terminal and airport train system, at a cost exceeding two billion dollars. We also built and refurbished facilities in Los Angeles, Atlanta, and Chicago, to name a few.

Part of my job included overseeing the company's headquarters facilities, reservation offices, aircraft hangars, and maintenance facilities. After a while, I became a walking book of airport and facility statistics and information. I could easily recount the number of gates we had at almost any airport we served, complete with a description of the location, rental rates, and the names of airlines occupying gates adjacent to ours. I committed to memory the number of square feet of office space we had in the headquarters buildings, along with the numbers of employees in each building. It was a dizzying array of information.

Given the magnitude of the company's construction projects, I had a lot of meetings and phone calls with Bob Crandall, who took over the chairman and CEO roles from Al Casey in 1985. My goal of becoming general counsel hadn't changed, and I knew doing a good job for Crandall just might be the ticket. He had a reputation for getting involved in the details, both big and small, of all aspects of running an airline. Nothing got past him. It drove managers of the company crazy, as it did me. Because airport terminals were often a first contact point for customers, I was on the receiving end of many "suggestions" from Crandall. Even when it involved a late-night call filled with complaints and a bunch of expletives, I couldn't help but admire his passionate drive for excellence.

While I was still working in the real estate department, one day I was summoned to Crandall's office to discuss an airport facility issue. His office was decorated simply, with a mixture of gray and white tones, no other color. At that time, there were large picture windows that looked over a large, flat, undeveloped field, with DFW Airport in the background. My office had a similar view and I kept a pair of binoculars in my desk drawer so I could watch coyotes trot across the field in search of their next meal.

Every meeting with Crandall was stressful. You never knew what topic he might raise or what complaint he might lodge. He liked it that way. As I stood up to leave, he said there was one more issue to discuss. Turns out, the old grandfather clock in the hallway outside his office was running a few minutes slow.

Crandall reminded me that American was the "on-time" machine and he said that we couldn't have a clock that didn't keep the correct time. "Either get it fixed or sell the damn thing," he growled.

The clock happened to be a rare antique given to C.R. Smith, another legendary former CEO, as a gift many years earlier. I nearly saluted as I scurried out of his office promising to get right on it.

I immediately called Suzanne Turner, who ran day-to-day campus facility issues. After I explained the problem, she had the clock sent to a master clock repairman in New York City, whose specialty was fixing antique grandfather clocks. Suzanne soon learned that the repairman was unable to fix the clock. He explained that clocks of its vintage always ran a few minutes slow. I had the clock shipped back and returned to its original spot outside Crandall's office.

Knowing that the clock would never keep the correct time, I came up with a plan. When the clock was returned, I arranged for Crandall's assistant to push the minute hand forward a few minutes each day before Crandall arrived. A few weeks later, as I prepared to walk out of Crandall's office following a meeting, he took me aside and said, "By the way, nice job on the clock. It keeps perfect time." I wasn't sure if it was a setup, so I responded with a confident, "Thanks, I'm glad it worked out." I breathed a sigh of relief. My plan had worked.

I was quite proud of myself for saving the clock and pulling a fast one on the boss. Only years later did I learn that Crandall actually knew what we were doing the entire time. Apparently, he got a good laugh over his double-cross maneuver.

I still desperately wanted to be general counsel, and I made sure that Don Carty—who replaced Crandall as chairman and CEO upon Crandall's 1998 retirement—was well aware of my interest. At one point, I sent a memo to Carty outlining my credentials in the event American's longtime general counsel, Anne McNamara, decided to leave.

My patience paid off when Anne surprised Carty, in late 2002, by announcing that she planned to retire. Her decision came at a difficult time. The company was in dire financial straits (in large part due to the events of 9/11), which meant that Carty needed to fill the job quickly.

Don Carty is a graduate of the Harvard Business School and has boundless amounts of energy. He is well over six feet tall, a bit gangly, with a shock of white hair that never quite stays in place. His voice is deep and marked by a Canadian accent. His ability to lead is evident by his natural charm and disarming demeanor. If he wasn't CEO, he could run for office. Don Carty knows how to work a room.

I liked Carty from the first day I met him. He was a whiz with numbers and could decipher detailed reports prepared by first-year analysts in a matter of minutes. Don's Canadian roots often made for a few laughs. In one meeting, some officers discussed the cost of painting a logo on an aircraft. Don listened to the presentation, then proposed that instead of painting the aircraft, the company should opt to use "deckles." "What's a deckle?" someone asked. "You know, a deckle," Carty responded impatiently. Finally someone piped in, "Oh, you mean a decal." "That's what I said, a deckle," Carty chuckled.

To my disbelief, within days of Anne McNamara's announced retirement, Carty called me to his office and asked if I was interested in the job of general counsel. I lowered my voice to suppress my delight and assured Carty that I was the right guy for the job and that I was ready to assume the role on a moment's notice. Carty, cautious, warned me that he planned to speak with a few other candidates. He assured me that he would make a quick decision.

I practically leaped as I left his office. Despite my excitement, I made a mental checklist of the possible candidates, both inside and outside the company. It felt great to be on the short list. How could Carty select anyone else for the job that I coveted for almost twenty years? But doubt persisted. All I could do was wait to see how things played out.

As the days passed, I watched for clues every time I saw McNamara or Carty. Once, I caught the two of them speaking in the hallway in hushed tones with someone I worried might be a contender for the job. I convinced myself that all was lost, and that I was destined to live out my days building airport terminals surrounded by architects and engineers. That wouldn't be a bad outcome, but one that would spell failure in my mind. I deserved to be general counsel, and Carty had to know that. Five days passed, then ten. Still no word. Carty had gone radio silent.

In January 2003, I planned to leave work early for a long weekend in Mexico with my family. Before I left my office, the phone rang. It was Carty's executive assistant, Carol Hess. She told me Carty wanted to speak with me in his office. Carol worked for Carty for many years and easily could have had a career as a champion poker player. I tried to read something from the tone of her voice and sheepishly asked if she knew what Carty wanted to see me about. Carol remained tight-lipped. I tried to remain calm and told her I would be right up.

My office was on the third floor. I rarely took the elevator, so I bounded up three flights of stairs as fast I could. By the time I got to the sixth floor I was out of breath and unable to carry on a conversation without sounding like I was ready to pass out. I stood at the top of the stairs and waited until my heart rate returned to normal, then walked through the executive wing and found Carol seated at her desk.

"He's waiting for you," she said. I swallowed hard and walked into Carty's office.

CHAPTER 2

TOUGH CHOICES

"Well, if you still want the job, I'd like you to be our next general counsel."

I couldn't believe my good fortune. I finally got the job I so desperately wanted. I accepted on the spot. No questions. No discussion. I didn't even ask about the salary or perks. I was all in.

Carty quickly tempered my enthusiasm. We were seated at a small table off to one side of his office. He seemed preoccupied as he gazed out the window at the aircraft departing and arriving at DFW Airport. Carty reiterated what I already knew about the company's financial condition and made it clear that it was going to be a bumpy ride. He told me that as general counsel I would be at the epicenter of the company's possible bankruptcy filing.

Carty then made one other remark, one that stuck with me all these years later. It was actually more of a question than a statement.

"You know, Gary, as general counsel you're going to have to stand up to me and be willing to tell me things that I don't want to hear." Carty paused. "Can you do that? Are you prepared to do that?"

Frankly, I hadn't given the issue much thought. I was so excited about finally getting the job I wanted for so long that I would have agreed to anything. Maybe it was the way he said it or his reflective tone, but I took note. What I didn't realize at the time is that

Carty's statement foreshadowed what was to come. In less than three months, his query would test both my professional and personal mettle in ways I never expected.

Reflecting on the challenges then facing the company, I'm a bit surprised that Carty offered me the job. He was the CEO of a company losing several millions of dollars a day and on a direct path to bankruptcy. He had just lost his longtime general counsel, and offered the job to me, the guy in charge of building airport terminals, an attorney who hadn't practiced law in twelve years.

Yet Carty somehow managed to convince the board of directors to support his choice for general counsel. If this scenario presented itself today, particularly given the focus on corporate governance, it is unlikely a board would approve the appointment. In the years following my promotion, I've thanked Don Carty many times for believing in me and for giving me the opportunity to lead the legal affairs of American Airlines.

My first day on the job as general counsel was January 27, 2003. And my first assignment was to prepare the necessary papers to place American Airlines and its parent company, AMR Corporation, into bankruptcy. If we filed, it would be the largest airline bankruptcy in history. It was almost inconceivable that American Airlines had fallen so precipitously. But there was little time to lament given the enormity of the task ahead. Exactly how we got to this point is a story in itself, but the basics are pretty straightforward.

Starting in 1990, American suffered four consecutive years of losses. Then, with some serious belt-tightening and an improving economy, the company returned to profitability in 1994. In fact, the seven years from 1994 through 2000 marked the most profitable period in the airline's history to that point. In the aggregate, the company reported a net income of 5.5 billion dollars, including two years—1996 and 1998—when American earned more than one billion dollars for the first time in its history. But this was the airline industry and the good times vanished almost overnight.

The year 2001 was marked by a perfect storm—a trifecta of events that placed the airline in a tailspin, the likes of which we had never experienced. The first event was of our own doing. The other two were beyond our control.

The first event involved Trans World Airlines, a company with a long history of problems and in the midst of another financial crisis. Despite its difficulties, the airline had a number of attractive assets, and American was anxious to capitalize on TWA's misfortune. In January 2001, TWA filed for bankruptcy and American swooped in and purchased their assets and most of their liabilities. The transaction closed in April 2001. The media heralded the deal as a brilliant strategy masterminded by Don Carty. The deal allowed American to substantially grow the airline overnight at a fraction of the cost of a traditional merger. We got 20,000 new employees, 190 additional aircraft, a new hub in St. Louis, and valuable landing slots at crowded airports, all at a bargain price.

The euphoria of the deal didn't last long. Within five months, American had a merger hangover, filled with regret and second-guessing. Rarely has a deal looked so bad in hindsight.

The second leg of the trifecta was not of our doing, though one could argue that we should have seen it coming. The airline business has always been highly cyclical. If the economy fired on all cylinders and the price of oil was stable, airlines made money. If the economy went south and oil prices spiked, airlines bled red ink like a stuck pig. In this case, the U.S. economy officially entered a recession in March 2001, just as we put the finishing touches on the TWA deal.

The final part of the trifecta marked one of the saddest days in U.S. history, and undoubtedly the worst day in the history of American Airlines—the terrorist attacks of September 11, 2001. The events of that tragic day began to unfold early that morning.

At approximately 7:30 a.m. Central Time, Gerard Arpey, then executive vice president of American's flight operations, called American's system operations control center (SOC). The SOC is responsible for coordinating all of American's flights around the world. Gerard wanted to let them know he had a scheduling conflict that prevented him from participating in the daily conference call (held each morning at 7:45). Joe Bertapelle, one of the SOC managers, answered the phone. Joe told Gerard that he had just tried to page him because of a possible hijacking on Flight 11, one of American's transcontinental flights.

Bertapelle said that the SOC manager on duty, Craig Marquis, was in contact with Betty Ong, one of American's flight attendants on that flight. Betty, located in the rear of the aircraft, used her cell phone to call American's reservations center in Raleigh, North Carolina, after the aircraft was hijacked. Betty's call was then patched through to the SOC.

Betty kept her composure as she reported that two flight attendants had been stabbed, along with one of the passengers in the first-class cabin. She also said that two or three of the hijackers were in the cockpit. Betty Ong was a true hero that day. Despite her fear, she remained professional as she described the events unfolding onboard the aircraft.

Arpey hurried out of the office and jumped in his car for the short ride to the SOC, a little over a mile from our Fort Worth headquarters. He arrived at approximately 7:35 a.m. Within minutes, he learned that an aircraft had crashed into the World Trade Center. By that time, communication with Betty Ong had been cut off. Gerard and Don Carty discussed the situation by telephone and Don asked Gerard if he knew whether the aircraft that hit the World Trade Center was, in fact, an AA aircraft. At that time, there was no official confirmation.

While trying to confirm the identity of the aircraft that had hit the World Trade Center, air traffic control officials confirmed that another of American's flights, Flight 77, was not responding to radio calls and that air traffic control could not determine its location. At this point, Arpey and his SOC colleagues decided to immediately stop any other flights from taking off in the Northeast corridor. A few minutes later, the decision to discontinue further takeoffs was expanded to include the entire American Airlines system.

Shortly thereafter, a second aircraft hit the World Trade Center. At that time, the SOC team believed that the second aircraft to crash into the World Trade Center may have been Flight 77. (In reality, the second aircraft to hit the World Trade Center was United Flight 175. American Flight 77 would later crash into the Pentagon). Arpey continued to confer with the SOC managers. Everyone believed that it was best to get all airborne American aircraft "on the deck" immediately.

At that point, Carty arrived at the Command Center. Gerard reviewed the situation with Don, and, without hesitation, Carty agreed that all airborne American and American Eagle flights should be diverted to the nearest suitable airports. This meant that hundreds of pilots in the air were forced to land immediately. This occurred at about 8:15 a.m. Central Time.

Carty then spoke by phone with FAA Administrator Jane Garvey. He told her of the decision to ground the entire American fleet and she asked him what he thought the FAA should do. Carty told Garvey that if it were his call, he would issue a nationwide ground stop. Two or three minutes later, that's exactly what happened. The FAA shut down the entire civil aviation system in the U.S., except for military aircraft. This was the first time such an order had ever been issued. It was an historic action.

For the remainder of the day, American's employees worked tirelessly to respond to the monumental logistical challenges that arose from the decision to shutter the U.S. civil aviation system. The next scheduled flights did not take off until several days after September 11, and the company did not have a full flight schedule for several more days.

The events of 9/11 were truly catastrophic. On that day, terrorists hijacked four aircraft—two American Airlines aircraft and two United Airlines aircraft. Nearly three thousand people were killed, including pilots, flight attendants, and other members of the American Airlines family.

For American Airlines, the events of 9/11 completed the trifecta—a badly timed airline acquisition, a recession, and a terrorist attack of unspeakable horror. These three events catapulted American into the worst financial crisis of its seventy-five-year history, one that American suffered for many years.

Other airlines were no better off. Between late 2001 and the end of 2005, airlines across the country, both large and small, were forced to seek bankruptcy protection, while others simply quit flying and disappeared. United Airlines filed for bankruptcy in December 2002; US Airways Group in August 2002 and again in September 2004; and both Delta Air Lines and Northwest Airlines in September 2005. Air Canada entered bankruptcy proceedings in April 2003. Aloha Airlines filed for bankruptcy in December 2004 and completely discontinued passenger service in 2008.

The events of 9/11 resulted in cataclysmic financial results for the airline industry. By 2003, American was swimming in a tide of red ink. In 2001 and 2002, American lost 5.3 billion dollars. The losses in those two years eviscerated the 5.5 billion dollars the airline earned between 1994 and 2000. Internally, we knew things were only going to deteriorate further. The company posted horrific results in the first quarter of 2003—a whopping one billion-dollar loss. These losses were rapidly diminishing our cash reserves and American faced a genuine cash-flow problem in the coming months.

Something had to be done and there was no time to waste. In a 2003 quarterly earnings call, Jeff Campbell, the CFO, summed up the situation in one simple sentence: "It's clear from the magnitude of losses we sustained this quarter and this year [referring to 4Q and full year 2002] that our current situation is not sustainable."

The solution was painful, yet obvious. American Airlines was on a direct path to the steps of the bankruptcy court. We simply had no other choice. It was the only viable option available, unless...unless we could somehow maneuver our way out of the hole we were in.

Would it be possible to convince our employees and vendors to provide wage and contractual concessions voluntarily? Concessions that would be roughly equivalent to the savings we could achieve in bankruptcy court? The conventional wisdom at the time was a resounding "No way."

On the one hand, achieving concessions from management and nonunionized employees is easy. You set targets and implement them. They are "at will" employees whose only recourse is to accept the changes or quit. But, it's an entirely different ballgame with labor.

Relations with the unions at American were bad, as they had been for many years. The flight attendants went on strike in

November 1993, and the pilots did the same in February 1997. The flight attendant strike lasted for five days and severely crippled the airline before President Clinton convinced management and the flight attendants to send their issues to binding arbitration, thereby ending the strike and saving the Thanksgiving travel season for millions of people. The pilot strike could easily have shut down the airline but, once again, President Clinton stepped in and enjoined the strike within minutes after it started by invoking his powers under the Railway Labor Act.

Despite the acrimonious relationship with labor, Don Carty firmly believed he could convince the unions to grant the deep wage and work rule concessions the company needed to avoid bankruptcy.

Carty's argument in favor of a voluntary restructuring was multilayered, but consisted largely of two overriding principles. First, a voluntary restructuring could be achieved in a matter of days, not the eighteen-plus months it would take to wind our way through the bankruptcy court system. Second, voluntary cuts provided both the company and labor a known outcome, one that removed the vagaries and uncertainties that are part of a court-imposed restructuring. For the company, it guaranteed the cuts we needed to survive and, for labor, certainty that the cuts would go no deeper than the agreed-upon concessions.

With the board firmly in support of his efforts, Carty and the senior executive team began work on a package of concessions. The most glaring question at the outset was pretty simple: How much do we ask for? The total "ask" needed to be large enough to give American a real opportunity to get back on its feet, but not so large that it would doom the effort from the outset. Chief financial officer Jeff Campbell, along with a ream of financial analysts, worked hand in hand with the Human Resources and Employee Relations departments to come up with the "ask." In February 2003, their work resulted in an outline of what American needed—two billion dollars annually.

We swallowed hard. It was an unprecedented number. Of the total, we needed 1.8 billion dollars in annual savings from employees—one billion dollars in the form of pay and benefits cuts and the

17

remaining eight hundred million dollars from work rules changes. The final two hundred million dollars was slated to come from vendors, lessors, and suppliers that did business with the company.

We told both groups that we needed a deal quickly or not at all. Lest anyone think we were kidding, we made our plans public. If we didn't achieve two billion dollars in concessions, we planned to file for bankruptcy on April 15, 2003. It was a race against the clock.

My mission at that time was crystal clear—be ready to file if the deadline passed without a deal. The work involved to prepare for a bankruptcy filing of this magnitude is extraordinary. Teams from virtually every department in the company worked night and day. As negotiations with the unions progressed, I was directing a legal juggernaut of attorneys, consultants, and bankers, all standing ready if Carty failed to get the concessions needed to save the airline. Armies of people from some of the most prestigious and expensive law firms in the country were billing tens of thousands of dollars a day drafting affidavits, motions, pleadings, reports, and memos.

To protect the secrecy of confidential projects, American often adopted code names. The preparations for bankruptcy were no longer secret, but we had a code name nonetheless. It was called Project Vermont. More than once, Carty asked why it was called Vermont. Most people at the company had no idea. Neither did I at the outset. I later learned it was derived from a financial analyst associating our consultant "Greenhill" with the Green Mountain range in Vermont.

As the self-imposed deadline of April 15 drew near with no concessionary agreements in hand, I prepared to fly to New York to file the bankruptcy papers. I made my reservation to fly from DFW to LaGuardia Airport. I arrived at the gate, sat down and waited for the boarding process to begin. After a few minutes, I heard the gate agent make an announcement:

"Passenger Gary Kennedy, if you are in the boarding area, please see the agent. Gary Kennedy, please see the agent prior to boarding."

I recall thinking the request a bit odd given that I was flying on a "positive space" ticket and already had my boarding pass. Employees who travel on company business are given varying levels of boarding priority, anywhere from a priority marginally better than "space available" all the way up to a first-class "positive space" ticket. A positive space ticket has the same status as a paying passenger. I approached the agent and gave her my name.

"Mr. Kennedy, we have an emergency situation. There is a woman traveling to New York, and it's imperative that we give her your seat on this flight. I assume you are OK with that."

"Sure. If you need the seat, that's fine," I told her.

"Thank you. Please wait in the boarding area for a moment."

I sat down and waited. Five minutes passed, then ten. Boarding was underway. Another announcement came from the gate agent. "Gary Kennedy, please see the agent. Mr. Gary Kennedy, please see the agent."

Once more, I approached the counter. "Yes, you called my name again." The agent's tone was serious. "Thank you, Mr. Kennedy. We no longer need your seat. You are free to board the aircraft." No further explanation was provided.

This was not the first time something like this occurred. We were accustomed to airport agents and other employees tracking the movements of senior officers. Typically, the tracking of flights and related gamesmanship was reserved for Don Carty and Gerard Arpey. I typically flew under the radar. But with labor negotiations in full swing and bankruptcy rumors swirling, this particular gate agent decided to try her hand at a little mischief.

A later investigation determined that the seating issue at the gate was entirely fabricated—there was no emergency or passenger who needed my seat. It turned out to be a misguided effort to keep me off the New York-bound flight under the mistaken idea that somehow it would delay a bankruptcy filing. I suspect it was the agent's way of venting her frustration with management. Today, it seems a bit humorous. At the time, I was not particularly amused.

I arrived in New York and went straight to the offices of Weil, Gotshal & Manges, our lead bankruptcy counsel. Weil was the premier bankruptcy shop in the country. They routinely handled many of the highest-profile bankruptcies and I knew them well. I moved into Weil's offices and worked nonstop reviewing and revising enormous numbers of documents and legal papers. The stress of the deadline and the gravity of the potential filing were smothering. The consequences of filing crowded my mind—thousands of people would lose their jobs, the company would be at the mercy of a judge and creditors' committees, and there was no certainty of a successful reorganization. Everything, including my future, was at stake. The pressure was on, but we plowed ahead for the next seventy-two hours.

Around 10 p.m. on the eve of the proposed filing, I was seated at a conference room table editing one of the bankruptcy documents. The senior partner in Weil's restructuring practice sat down and said we needed to discuss an urgent matter. She told me that the firm simply did not have a sufficient retainer from American and that we needed to wire additional funds before the case was filed. Law firms handling bankruptcy cases always take big retainers because once a filing is made, all legal fees must be approved by the court. However, this last-minute request took me by surprise.

I could hardly contain my annoyance. "Why are we discussing this now? Why didn't we hear about this long before?"

She slid her chair away from the table and told me that the case was getting more complicated by the day and that the firm was spending a lot more money than originally envisioned. We had already given the firm millions of dollars as an advance on legal fees. I was tired and in no mood to talk about fees late the night before the filing. She then told me that the firm needed a substantial sum of additional money wired to the firm's account first thing in the morning.

I got out of my chair, told her I needed to discuss it with my guys and would get back to her. I then found Kathy Koorenny. Kathy was my associate general counsel and the person responsible for the day-to-day bankruptcy planning. Kathy had an angelic face and military style haircut. Her personality matched the latter. I quickly filled her in on the conversation. Her response was vintage Kathy: "No way are we giving them more money."

We both knew that wasn't true, but it felt good to say it. We wired the money the next morning. I understood the firm's rationale. They were spending tremendous amounts of time and money on our case, and it would be several months down the road before a judge would approve additional payments to the firm. Nevertheless, it was disheartening and poorly timed.

The deadline for filing arrived. A full entourage of AA executives were assembled in a conference room at Weil, including Jeff Campbell, Kathy Koorenny, Bev Goulet, vice president of corporate development and treasurer, and a host of attorneys, paralegals, bankers, financial analysts, and consultants. We were all waiting. Waiting for a call from Don Carty letting us know if his last-ditch efforts to get a deal with labor paid off or if we were headed to court.

It was getting late and we had to arrive at the federal bankruptcy courthouse before they closed. It was after 3 p.m. We were pacing. I began to think that Carty had failed. We made the decision to stage the boxes of bankruptcy documents by the elevators, readying for the trip to the courthouse. In those days, there was no such thing as an electronic filing of pleadings. We had reams of court filings stacked in boxes. The amount of paper was almost cartoonish. We used two-wheeled dollies and strapped the boxes with bungee cords. In preparation for the dash to the courthouse, limousines were lined up on Fifth Avenue standing by.

Sometime around 3:30 p.m., Jeff got a call from Carty. The news was a mixed bag. The pilots and the Transport Workers Union (TWU) voted to accept the package of concessions, but 51 percent of the flight attendants voted to reject it. Instead of filing as we had threatened, Carty made the decision to extend the deadline by one day. Fearful that a Chapter 11 filing would result in demands for even larger concessions, the flight attendant leadership announced that they would allow those who had already voted to change their vote.

The next day, we once again found ourselves waiting to see if we had a deal. Late that evening, we learned our fate. The flight attendants voted to approve the deal with 52 percent in favor. We all breathed easier, believing the worst was behind us.

Of course, our relief was premature. The real drama was yet to unfold. This new drama tested the resilience of the company, its board of directors, and its CEO. For me, it tested the question Don Carty posed to me just months before—could I tell him things he didn't want to hear?

CHAPTER 3

TROUBLE AT THE TOP

The drama began on April 16, 2003, shortly after we filed our 10-K annual report and the same day that the flight attendant votes were counted. Annual reports are boring and few people read them, other than Wall Street analysts and industry reporters. But the 2003 10-K had a hidden land mine that exploded in American's face.

The 10-K is a lengthy document that the Securities and Exchange Commission (SEC) requires public companies to file each year. It provides investors with a comprehensive summary of the company's financial performance. In addition, the document contains disclosures about compensation paid to senior executives of the company as well as contracts or promises to pay executives in the future.

Exhibit 10.59 of the 10-K contained a short section that read as follows:

> *In consideration of the Officer remaining an employee of the Corporation from March 1, 2002, through and including January 31, 2005 (the "Retention Period"), the Corporation will pay to the Officer a Cash Retention Bonus.*

The document went on to spell out that the bonus would be paid to a handful of top executives if they stuck around—half in early 2004 and the other half in early 2005. The recipients, like Don

Carty, Gerard Arpey, and myself, were to receive a bonus equal to two times our base salary. Others were to receive the same amount or something less, like 1.5 times base salary.

There was a second statement in the 10-K focused on a supplemental employee retirement plan referred to as a SERP. That statement detailed a 41 million-dollar payment into a pension trust for the benefit of officers of the company. This trust was set up to be secure even if we filed for bankruptcy. It is a common tool used to pay executives a pension benefit in circumstances when their pension exceeds the maximum amount that can be paid under federal pension laws. American established the SERP many years earlier but never deposited money into the account, choosing instead to pay the remainder of an executive's pension benefits out of the company's general revenues. As the company got into serious financial difficulty after 9/11, the board of directors decided it was prudent to deposit funds into the SERP trust so that the pensions of executives would be protected, just as they are for other company employees under federal law.

About a week before we filed the 10-K, Jeff Campbell and I discussed the timing of the filing with Carty. Jeff is a paper-thin guy who is near genius in his abilities. What he lacks in body mass he makes up for in smarts and strong opinions. Campbell believed that the 10-K was ready to be filed with the SEC and that it should be filed before the unions voted. Carty disagreed that the 10-K was complete and thought that disclosure prior to the union vote was a bad idea: "Why in the world would we lead with our chin? We've got to get these concessions approved."

Jeff and I understood Carty's view. It was essential that we save the company from bankruptcy and avoid doing anything that put the union votes at risk. But, we remained concerned about the timeliness of the 10-K disclosure.

Tensions surrounding the issue continued to escalate. Campbell's frustration erupted in a private meeting among Arpey, Bev Goulet, Jeff, and me. We were in Gerard's office and continued to debate the issue. As the discussion wound down, Campbell uttered a choice expletive, then hurled his fountain pen across the room. I watched it rocket out of his hand, bounce once, then slam with great force into the opposite wall. From the look on Jeff's face, I think he was as surprised as the rest of us at the sheer velocity of the pen.

Hell hath no fury like a labor union scorned. In this case, the fury came within minutes after labor leaders read the 10-K. Everything that Carty worked so hard to achieve was now in jeopardy. The disclosure that certain officers and executives at the company were set to receive retention bonuses and pension benefits under the SERP roiled the unions. How could management receive millions of dollars of payments while employees sacrificed 1.8 billion dollars in annual wages and benefits? In their view, the wool had been pulled over their eyes. They believed they had been lied to and deceived by management.

Carty reminded the union leaders that months earlier he had shared with them his concern that the continued deterioration of the company's financial performance was driving officers to leave the company at alarming rates, and that he needed to take action to stem the tide. He had also told them that he had instituted a program to entice certain officers to remain with the company during the difficult times. Carty's explanation fell on deaf ears.

We hoped that labor leaders would acknowledge that Carty had, in fact, given them advance notice of these payments. We wanted them to tell their members that, like it or not, the retention payments to officers were necessary. But we knew such an acknowledgment would be political suicide, particularly when their members were giving up so much.

As the details disclosed in the 10-K became widely known, matters grew more urgent as the unions cried foul and demanded that American reopen negotiations on the concessionary package. The unions wanted to rewrite the deal before the ink was dry on the first deal. The flight attendants went one step further. The Association of Professional Flight Attendants (APFA) announced a decision to rescind the earlier vote approving the concessionary agreements. They planned to have a revote on the concession package. It was total chaos. No one knew exactly what to expect or what could be done to get the concessions back on track and the company moving forward.

Carty quickly tried to make peace with labor. The first thing he decided was to ditch the retention payments. But these agreements were contracts with each individual officer so he needed each officer to consent to the rescission. One after another, Don called his officers and asked for their consent. Don called me on Saturday morning, April 19. It was a short discussion. I knew what he needed me to do, and I immediately gave him my OK.

When I hung up the phone, I looked at my wife. "Well, we just lost three-quarters of a million dollars in two minutes."

"Wow, that was an expensive call," my wife remarked with a sarcastic tone. "You may not want to answer the phone if Don calls again."

The decision to relinquish the bonus payments did not solve the problem. Labor remained angry, and the concessionary deals remained in jeopardy. With all the uncertainty, we were forced to restart the bankruptcy preparation machine. As a potential filing moved forward, an even larger drama was underway inside the boardroom.

With the company hemorrhaging red ink, employees angry, customers uncertain about the future of the airline, Wall Street shaking its head in disbelief, and regulators circling like vultures, the temperature inside the boardroom was at a boiling point. As general counsel, it was my job to moderate that temperature and calm the waters. It was also my responsibility to advise the board regarding its fiduciary obligations and guide them in their deliberations.

My stomach was in knots about what loomed ahead. A lot of good a hard hat and all the construction experience was doing for me now. I was in the deep end of the ocean, unsure how I would manage to stay afloat.

As the upheaval swirled and the prospects of a satisfactory outcome dimmed, I reached a difficult conclusion, one that, for me, felt akin to treason—I had a duty to speak privately with our board and raise the prospect that Carty may have to resign as CEO.

Don took a huge risk naming me as general counsel and I felt indebted to him. Yet, as the company's chief legal officer, I had an obligation to advise our board that they may need to replace him. I was conflicted then, and I feel the same today. Don Carty had the company's best interests top of mind at all times. He was planning for the future when he made the decision to create a pension trust and adopt retention agreements for senior management, a common practice to ensure strong management when a company is in financial distress.

Carty's disclosure to union leadership was above board, but didn't go nearly far enough. He should have told them exactly what retention programs he put in place and how much money was at stake. The problem was that the leaders were put on their heels when the 10-K was made public. Faced with angry union members, the leadership turned the issue into a disclosure debacle they quickly hung on Carty. Their position was understandable. The optics of the situation were horrible. Employees had given billions of dollars in concessions and work rule changes while management looked like they were lining their pockets with bundles of cash.

Late in the afternoon on April 21, I told Don that I needed to speak privately with the board the next morning. I shared the subject matter—his continued role as CEO of the airline. Don didn't miss a beat. He said something to the effect of, "No problem, I understand." And that was it. He had no intention of interfering with my job in any way.

Late that evening, I sat alone in my office outlining what I planned to say to the board. It was a delicate subject, and I knew I had to get it right. It was close to 9:30 p.m. as I struggled with my talking points. I needed to bounce it off someone. Even though it was an hour later in New York, I called Rich Rothman, a senior litigation partner at Weil Gotshal. Rothman is a close friend and someone I grew to rely upon for advice when difficult problems arose. I laid out the situation to Rich, and he immediately got Greg Danilow on the phone with us. Danilow is a governance expert with the firm. With their help, I honed the outline for the board call.

The next morning, April 22, with the entire board assembled on the call, I outlined their fiduciary responsibilities. I also reviewed the facts as we knew them to be, along with those factors, both pro and con, that the board needed to consider as they debated Carty's continued role as CEO. The board members asked a few clarifying questions and thanked me for my candor and advice.

Unbeknownst to me, Carty had already made the decision to resign. On April 23, the day after my meeting with the board, Carty had lengthy discussions with labor leaders and several members of Congress from North Texas. Always the strategic planner, Carty used his forthcoming resignation as a lever to convince labor leaders to accept the concessionary packages. That same night, Carty had dinner at the Hilton Anatole with a handful of AA board members, including Ed Brennan, Phil Purcell, and Mike Miles. He told them of his plan to resign. Although certain members of the board believed that Carty should resign, those at dinner were not pleased with his decision.

On April 24, 2003, American announced that Don Carty would resign, effective immediately. Gerard Arpey was named president and CEO, and board member Ed Brennan was named executive chairman. In a statement issued as part of the announcement, Carty acknowledged that his departure was needed to heal the wounds with labor:

> It is now clear that my continuing on as Chairman and CEO of American Airlines is still a barrier that, if removed, could give improved relations—and thus long-term success—the best possible chance. So today, to remove that barrier and to help make possible the success American's employees so richly deserve, the AMR board of directors has accepted my offer to step down as Chairman and CEO of American Airlines.

And, he added, "It is my fervent hope that my resignation and the appointment of Ed and Gerard will enable the company, its unions and its employees to begin to build a bridge back to the path that promised a new culture of collaboration, cooperation and trust."

With Carty's resignation behind us, the second APFA vote was announced on Friday, April 25. We won—they narrowly approved a revised package of concessions. The immediate crisis was over. But not for long. As we warned in our 10-K filing ten days earlier, the company was in a precarious position:

> *Even if the Labor Agreements are ratified and the Company obtains concessions from its vendors, lessors and suppliers, the Company may nonetheless need to initiate a Chapter 11 filing because its financial condition will remain weak and its prospects uncertain.*

The company's future remained in doubt. So much so that the debate about the wisdom of filing for bankruptcy, despite the concessions, was still very much in play. Just minutes away from American's headquarters, at the Hilton Anatole in Dallas, Gerard Arpey, his senior management team, and the board, along with outside counsel and consultants, were in the midst of a spirited debate regarding what lie ahead for a downtrodden American Airlines.

CHAPTER 4

THE TURNAROUND PLAN

The debate underway in late April 2003 at the Hilton Anatole near downtown Dallas was akin to an HBO pay-per-view boxing match. No one wore gloves but everyone in the room was looking for that left jab or uppercut to the chin that would seal victory and bring closure to the question at hand. The question was simple: Despite labor's approval of the concessions, should American Airlines file for bankruptcy anyway?

The answer seemed obvious. The company asked for and received nearly two billion dollars of concessions from labor and vendors. Achieving the concessions had been incredibly difficult, with all sides doing what they could to save the airline from bankruptcy. That should have saved us, right?

But the airline business is notoriously complicated, and so too was our next move. The company was on life support, with barely enough cash to stay afloat. The labor force was fractured and angry. Management had a new chairman, a new CEO, and a management team that was tired and worn thin. Even if we pushed forward, there was a low probability that we could avoid bankruptcy.

The most difficult problem facing the company was the shortage of cash. At that moment, American had less than 1.3 billion dollars of unrestricted cash. For a seventeen billion-dollar company that was hemorrhaging roughly 10 million dollars per day (based on first quarter operating losses), the level of cash reserves was frighteningly low. We were scraping the bottom of the barrel.

But, what about the concessions? Wouldn't they quickly remedy the cash crunch? Unfortunately, not in the short term. In fact, because the concessions were slated to "roll in" over a period of many months, and in some cases the benefits wouldn't be realized for a year or more, the concessions provided little immediate relief.

In one corner of the boxing ring, wearing Armani suits and gold cufflinks, stood the advisors and consultants to the company, principally bankers and lawyers. In the other corner, wearing the red and blue colors of the airline, were the CEO and senior officers. The judges responsible for rendering the final decision, preferably a unanimous one, were the twelve members of the board of AMR Corporation, the parent of American Airlines.

The decision to place a company under the protection of the bankruptcy laws lies entirely with its board of directors. It is their decision alone that counts. They must affirmatively vote to file for bankruptcy. Our board understood the grave nature of its responsibilities and undertook its mission with the utmost care and caution. Rarely in these circumstances is there a right or wrong answer. Under the "Business Judgment Rule," the law protects a board in its deliberative process, and its decisions will not be second-guessed by the courts so long as the board acts in good faith and on an informed basis.

Few people see firsthand what actually transpires inside a boardroom of a major U.S. corporation. Most should consider themselves lucky to have avoided the experience. Given the issue under discussion at this meeting, and the legal implications underpinning the decision, for me, this meeting was an intellectual adrenaline rush. The stakes were high, and the mood tense, as a cadre of lawyers and bankers laid out the pros and cons of filing. As they are prone to do, there was a generous helping of "on the one hand" and "on the other hand." After listening patiently for what seemed an eternity, the board drew an end to the discourse. They asked each consultant and senior officer to take an unequivocal stand—for or against filing for bankruptcy.

Two of the first people to speak were Harvey Miller and Bob Greenhill, both of Greenhill and Co., our investment banker. Even though Harvey was at that moment acting in the capacity as an investment bank restructuring advisor, he had been the country's preeminent bankruptcy attorney during his thirty-two years at Weil Gotshal. He joined Greenhill only after resigning from the law firm the previous year. Had he not resigned, there is no doubt we would have hired him as our lead bankruptcy counsel. In a strange twist of fate, Harvey would later return to Weil Gotshal and play a prominent role in American's 2011 bankruptcy filing.

Regarding the question before the house, both advisors advocated for an immediate filing. In fact, both Harvey Miller and Bob Greenhill stated vociferously that there was no viable alternative short of filing. They argued that any delay would only further damage the company and increase the risk of insolvency.

The senior officers then voiced their opinions. The vast majority disagreed with the outside consultants and believed a filing would only compound our problems. When asked to speak, I sided with my fellow officers, and told the board that a filing would lead to chaos and anarchy among employees. I distinctly recall using the word "anarchy" to describe the state in which the company would find itself if we pushed aside the concessions and filed for bankruptcy. Although it sounded dramatic, I meant it. American had a tough history with its employees, and I knew a filing would trigger adverse employee actions. I believed that employees would openly revolt against management, resulting in work stoppages and a hellish operating environment for our customers.

Most of the senior officers were twenty-year-plus veterans of the airline, and it was difficult for us to imagine that it was in the best interest of any constituency to file. Besides, I argued that if the concessionary route didn't work, we could still file at a later date.

I said so despite my knowledge of the first commandment of bankruptcy: "Thou shalt not wait too long." I spent my early days as a bankruptcy practitioner in Salt Lake City and witnessed firsthand what happens when companies drain their assets while hoping things will work out. But on this day, I was convinced that throwing in the towel was the wrong thing to do.

The new CEO of the airline, Gerard Arpey, was adamantly opposed to bankruptcy, a view he steadfastly maintained during his nearly nine-year tenure at the helm of the airline. The notion that a company would voluntarily place its future in the hands of a judge, creditors' committees, lawyers, and bankers, was, in his mind, unconscionable. Gerard's position was also in part a moral one. He never wavered from his belief that companies should honor their obligations and pay their debts as they become due. He simply could not countenance the notion that a company would walk away from its commitments to shareholders, creditors, and employees.

After considering the vast number of opinions put before them, the board unanimously decided to give the concessions a chance to work. There would be no bankruptcy filing. At least not on this day. We all breathed a sigh of relief. It felt like the right thing to do, but we knew the road ahead was going to be rough.

Arpey was now faced with an extraordinary task. He had to find a path forward for American, and he had to do so quickly. Gerard once described his appointment as CEO as tantamount to a "battlefield promotion." He knew the financial struggles were serious and that the acrimonious relationship with our labor groups could ruin the airline. As Gerard's general counsel, I was going to be standing next to him on that battlefield, and I hoped we had a fighting chance to come out of it alive.

Arpey started his career at American Airlines as a low-level financial analyst in 1982. He fit the mold of an AA executive perfectly—tall, thin, straitlaced, with a penchant for long work hours. Almost immediately, Gerard caught the eye of Bob Crandall, and he moved up the corporate ladder with lightning speed. Arpey was promoted to vice president in the finance organization before the age of thirty and became a senior vice president just a few years later. It was a remarkable rise. Arpey built a corporate fiefdom that expanded every few years until Carty named him president of the airline in 2002.

All told, Arpey and I worked together for almost thirty years and I know him well. Arpey is first and foremost a man of principle. There was no one more dedicated to American Airlines and its employees than Gerard Arpey.

The relationship between a CEO and his or her general counsel is unique. It is one that, at its core, must be grounded in mutual trust and a common set of values. Together, Gerard and I made a pact. First, we agreed that we would always do the right thing for our constituencies—employees, shareholders, lenders, and customers. Second, and equally important, we promised one another that we would always tell the truth, regardless of the fallout or consequences. The difficulties and challenges we faced over the next eight years tested this pact time and again.

Shortly after his election as CEO, Arpey called a meeting of his executive team. This team was comprised of a dozen of the most senior officers of the company. We gathered in Arpey's conference room located across the hall from his office. Inside the conference room is a large triangular table, with a chair designated for the CEO and one for each senior officer. At the time, it was known as the map room. This is the same room where, for the previous fifteen years, all major decisions of the company were debated, starting with Bob Crandall, then Don Carty, and now Gerard Arpey.

Arpey wasted little time getting to the point. We needed a mission statement—a simple, straightforward statement setting forth the principal goals that must be achieved for the airline to survive and prosper. It had to be something that employees could rally around, that Wall Street could buy into, and that would restore customer confidence. We debated the statement for three weeks, knowing we planned to roll it out during the Annual Meeting of shareholders set for May 21, 2003, at our training and conference center across the highway from our Fort Worth headquarters. Considering the state of the company, the mission statement was aptly named the "Turnaround Plan."

The Turnaround Plan consisted of four basic principles:

1. Lower Costs to Compete
2. Fly Smart, Give Customers What They Value
3. Pull Together, Win Together
4. Build a Financial Foundation for Our Future

The first tenet of the plan, "Lower Costs to Compete," was an admission that our costs remained too high, despite new concessionary labor agreements, and that we needed to find ways to drive our costs lower. The second tenet, "Fly Smart, Give Customers What They Value," focused on our customer base. We decided years earlier to curtail spending on most customer-related enhancements because we lacked the financial resources to do so. Consequently, customer satisfaction was poor, and we desperately needed to improve our product offering.

The third tenet of the Plan, "Pull Together, Win Together," a seemingly innocuous statement, was designed to repair our damaged relationship with employees and rally them to a shared vision of the future. The fourth tenet, "Build a Financial Foundation for Our Future," was directed both to Wall Street and our employees. We needed to convince employees that a robust financial foundation was essential to long-term success, and prove to Wall Street that we could recover from our financial malaise.

Progress under the first, second, and fourth tenets of the Plan was relatively easy to measure. The same was not true of the third tenet. When the Turnaround Plan was announced during the Annual Meeting, relations with organized labor were at an all-time low. After forking over more than 1.6 billion dollars in annual wage and work rule concessions (reduced from 1.8 billion dollars to convince labor to accept the concessions), they were in no mood to "Pull Together" with management, and they certainly did not trust that labor and management could ever "Win Together." After all, this was just a month removed from the outrage over the retention bonuses and pension trust that led to Don Carty's departure from the company.

Gerard was acutely aware of the depth of the challenge. He staunchly believed that honesty, integrity, and conviction of principle would lead to a renewed relationship with organized labor, one grounded in mutual respect and common purpose. In an effort to build trust with labor, Arpey refused to accept a pay increase at the time of his election as CEO (despite the fact that he and other top executives took substantial pay cuts shortly after 9/11). He also refused to accept the board's generous award of stock (set to vest in 2006).

Gerard embarked on his quest with labor by inviting them to join him in a new dialogue. He promised to meet with labor leaders on a regular basis and share with them detailed information about the company, its challenges and strategic plans. He agreed to consult with them and seek their input before embarking on major initiatives.

In essence, he wanted them to get off the sidelines and become part of the team.

Labor reluctantly accepted Gerard's invitation. For the first time in the company's history, the camel would have a lot more than just its nose under the tent; it would be inside the tent itself.

Arpey gave Jeff Brundage, our senior vice president of human resources, the task of figuring out exactly how all of this would work. In a former life, Brundage had been a pilot at Atlantic Coast Airlines and worked for the largest pilot union in the world, the Air Line Pilots Association (ALPA). ALPA represented the pilots of all our major competitors. Jeff had turned from airline pilot into a skilled union negotiator and advocate. He had a knack for working with pilots because he understood their issues. It was a coup that American lured him away from ALPA. He was honest and always thinking outside the box.

The assignment from Gerard was smack in the middle of Brundage's wheelhouse. Jeff set to work organizing a number of new committees and setting up a series of meetings with each labor union. He also reached out to the nonunionized workforce (principally airport ticket agents and reservation agents). Even the names given to the committees, like the Joint Leadership Team (JLT), the Joint Business Education Committee (JBEC), and the Agent Advisory Board (AAB), evoked a sense of unity and cooperation between management and rank and file employees.

The extent to which we agreed to share information with labor really hit home when each union participant, along with their legal and financial advisors, was required to sign nondisclosure agreements. By signing such agreements, they were entitled to receive the airline's "material nonpublic information." In other words, they were about to learn the ingredients of the secret sauce.

Initially, labor was skeptical of the newfound openness. They didn't truly believe that Arpey would follow through as promised. But Arpey was deeply committed to the process. Nothing about it was mere lip service. Slowly, as Gerard demonstrated that he truly wanted management and the unions to work together as partners, labor began to change its tune and concluded that the promise Arpey made was genuine.

While Arpey advanced his labor relations agenda, he looked to me to resolve a delicate governance issue. When Arpey was named president and CEO of American Airlines in April 2003, the board named Ed Brennan, then lead director, as executive chairman. Presumably, the board believed that separating the roles during a time of crisis would create a greater sense of stability inside the company and with external constituents, including Wall Street. Additionally, the board was cognizant of the fact that Arpey was new to the job and might benefit from Brennan's experience and governance expertise.

Ed Brennan was the former chairman, president, and CEO of Sears, Roebuck & Co. He retired from Sears after thirty-nine years. Brennan also sat on several corporate boards, including McDonald's Corporation, Exelon Corporation, and 3M Company. He joined American's board in 1987 and served on the board for twenty years before his retirement at age seventy-three. Brennan was held in high esteem in the business world as a true expert in matters involving corporate governance. He was the quintessential picture of the wise, gray-haired executive, in a crisp white shirt and dark blue suit. But what made Brennan stand apart was his friendly, down-to-earth demeanor, and the kindness he showed to everyone, regardless of position or stature.

When Brennan was named executive chairman in April 2003 (at the same time that Arpey assumed the role of CEO), we didn't really know exactly what Brennan's role would be, or how it would evolve. Arpey was busy doing everything he could to keep the company afloat and didn't have time to devote to the question. Besides, the decision to split the roles was one made quickly given the exigencies of the situation, and the board didn't have the luxury of carefully defining how Brennan and Arpey would divide responsibilities.

Ed lived full-time in Chicago and decided to spend one day each week (typically Monday) at our headquarters office. Knowing that Brennan's schedule for his weekly visits would be wide open, Arpey and I set up meetings between Ed and various senior officers on a broad range of subjects. Those meetings included in-depth financial and operational reviews, along with updates regarding our employee engagement efforts. Arpey always set aside a significant amount of time to meet individually with Brennan at some point during each of his visits.

This arrangement continued for several months, but as time went on and the business began to stabilize, Arpey and I concluded that the arrangement was becoming a bit awkward. It's not that Ed did anything wrong. To the contrary, he remained pleasant and supportive at all times. It was difficult for him, like it would be for any outside director, to make a meaningful contribution to the daily affairs of the company. We found ourselves expending significant resources preparing for Brennan's weekly visits, resources that could have been devoted to running the business. We also found that the division of leadership created uncertainty among employees, often leaving them in a state of confusion about who was running the company.

By definition, an executive chairman—as opposed to a nonexecutive chairman—is the top executive in the company. But Brennan's limited role and presence merely confused the issue. Was he in charge of running the company? Or was Gerard Arpey in charge, with Brennan looking benignly over Arpey's shoulder?

Early in 2004, just nine months after the board separated the roles of chairman and CEO, Arpey and I concluded that it was time to reverse course and seek board approval to consolidate both roles under Arpey's leadership. I reminded Gerard that our effort would run contrary to the position being advocated by shareholder activists and governance experts. I told him there was a big move afoot in corporate America to push companies to separate the chairman and CEO positions. Those commentators argued then, and do so today, that an independent chair improves the board's ability to monitor and oversee management. Those who favor a unified chairman/CEO model counter that consolidating the two positions leads to strong, central leadership and superior decision-making.

In a curious twist of fate, Brennan debated the pros and cons of separating the roles of chairman and CEO in a panel discussion with former Federal Reserve Chairman Paul Volker at a directors' institute in Chicago in April 2003, the same month he became executive chairman at American. Ironically, Brennan voiced concern about a director serving as chairman, warning that "I think you'd find too many directors...who want to be the co-CEO."

Thanks in large part to deft behind-the-scenes discussions among the board members, and directly with Brennan, Arpey received the green light to proceed with the proposed change at the upcoming May board meeting. While this wasn't really a battle for control, we had some concern that the outside world would view it that way. Ed was at the end of his career and wanted to help Gerard in any way he could. He was not interested in running the company. This was Gerard's moment and everyone knew it.

However, several days before the May board meeting, Gerard walked into my office with a look of concern crossing his face. "I'm not sure I can go through with this," he said.

I knew what he was talking about without asking. "Yes, you can. We have to. I know it's an unpopular move in some circles, but the current arrangement isn't working. We need to move ahead and get this done."

I think Gerard just needed a bit of reassurance. "Look, I know you're right, but it's hard to do this to someone like Ed," Gerard said. "He is such a great guy."

"This isn't about Ed," I replied. "You and I both know it's about what's best for the company. Besides, Ed understands that and he'll be fine."

Gerard nodded in agreement. "All right. Full speed ahead."

As planned, the board of directors took formal action at their May 18, 2004, meeting, adding the title of chairman to Arpey's existing duties as president and CEO of the airline. Ed Brennan graciously stepped down as chairman and accepted a new role as lead director. The changes were announced publicly the next morning at the company's Annual Meeting of Shareholders.

Adding the title of chairman to Arpey's duties did nothing to lessen the burden he faced as the company maneuvered its way through a minefield of difficult issues. It was time to get back to the vexing problem of how to fairly compensate his management team. Like Carty before him, Arpey knew that management compensation was well below market and had been for many years. Already, top executives were retiring early or leaving to take higher paying jobs.

For example, the position of chief financial officer was like a revolving door at a busy department store. Tom Horton was promoted to the CFO job in January 2000 and resigned in June 2002 to accept a better paying job at AT&T Corporation. His successor, Jeff Campbell, lasted only eighteen months before he accepted a more lucrative position at McKesson Corporation, a major pharmaceutical company. James Beer was next at bat and he stayed in the CFO job for less than fourteen months before leaving early in 2006 to join Symantec Corporation.

Just like the executive compensation issues that led to Carty's resignation in 2003, executive compensation played a leading role as events unfolded during Arpey's tenure as CEO.

There is a fundamental difference between the way management and nonmanagement employees are compensated. Most nonmanagement employees are paid an hourly wage, plus overtime. For airline employees, particularly pilots and flight attendants, the formula is a bit more complicated because of union contracts, but by and large they are paid for the number of in-flight hours worked. In addition to hourly wages, nonmanagement employees typically participate in a profit-sharing plan.

While the specifics of American's profit-sharing plan changed over the years, employees received payouts only if the company earned a threshold level of profits for the year in question. In 2003, American's plan called for a profit-sharing pool equal to 15 percent of all pretax earnings in excess of five hundred million dollars. In other words, American had to earn at least that amount before profit sharing would kick in. If earnings were less than five hundred million dollars, there would be no payout.

Management compensation is a different structure entirely. Management employees are paid an annual base salary instead of an hourly wage. And, for officers and top executives of most large U.S. corporations, base salary accounts for a relatively small percentage of overall compensation. For them, total compensation is comprised of a combination of fixed and variable components. The fixed component is the base salary and typically makes up about 30 to 40 percent of total compensation. The variable piece is comprised of a variety of cash bonus and equity-based awards, like stock options, performance-based stock, and restricted stock. If the awards pay out, they can account for 70 percent or more of total compensation. Similar to the profit-sharing plan for nonmanagement employees, top management employees receive cash bonuses only if the company is profitable.

What many people don't understand is that executive compensation does not fall under the purview of the CEO. It is the company's board of directors that has direct responsibility to set compensation for executive officers, including the CEO. In 2003 and beyond, American's board was painfully aware that the 2003 "retention payment" debacle remained a festering wound and that future payments to top executives would receive close scrutiny by labor unions.

As the board navigated the compensation minefield, it took into consideration a number of competing issues. On one side of the ledger, the board recognized that labor had sacrificed billions of dollars in annual givebacks and that Arpey was doing everything possible to regain labor's trust. On the flip side, the board recognized, as a matter of good corporate governance, that it needed to establish compensation plans designed to reward performance and retain senior executives. Each year, the board's compensation philosophy was detailed in AMR Corporation's SEC filing on Form 10-K.

Despite the turmoil in 2003, the compensation policies remained substantially similar from one year to the next. The reason for this is quite simple. The objectives of the AMR board, like the objectives of so many other large company boards, were designed to link management performance to the company's long-term strategic goals. If the company did well, the executives leading the company should be compensated accordingly.

In keeping with this philosophy, the final compensation plan adopted by the board in 2003, and for several years thereafter, was comprised of four essential elements: base salary; annual bonus based on company financial performance; stock options; and restricted stock (or stock-based units) with a three-year vesting schedule, also known as the Performance Unit Plan ("PUP").

As we soon learned, the Performance Unit Plan was the Achilles' heel to Arpey's "Pull Together, Win Together" mantra. It doomed his great experiment with labor and set in motion events that culminated in American's bankruptcy filing in 2011.

CHAPTER 5

UPRISING

With the labor agreements in place by late April 2003, the company began a painstaking process to pull itself from the edge of the cliff, one inch at a time. Slowly, American's operating performance began to improve and customer confidence in the future of the airline returned. The big question was how Wall Street would react to our efforts. We were not disappointed. Wall Street liked what it saw. AMR's stock bottomed out at $1.41 per share in March 2003. That year, we lost 1.2 billion dollars. A year later, we narrowed the loss to just under nine hundred million dollars and our stock closed at $10.95 on December 31, 2004.

As we marched forward with the recovery, the price of AMR stock continued to reflect our improving financial performance. The big news came in 2006 when we recorded a net profit—189 million dollars on revenues of 22.6 billion dollars. That calculated to a net return of only 1 percent, a miniscule return to investors, but it was the first profit in six years so we were pleased. Things got even better in 2007 as profits climbed to 456 million dollars.

As profits rose, so did the price of AMR stock. It hit a high of $40.66 in January 2007. While it was a gratifying development, there was a big problem lurking beneath the surface of the meteoric rise in the value of the stock. Under the compensation plans approved by the board in 2003 and in following years, as the price of the stock rose, top executives stood to make large sums of money under the "restricted stock" portion of the plan, creating a chasm with labor as deep and wide as the Grand Canyon.

Simply put, our executives and upper-level managers, several hundred in all, would earn equity-based awards according to how well the shares of parent AMR Corporation performed compared to the shares of other U.S. carriers, like Delta Air Lines, United Airlines, and Continental Airlines. The better our stock performed, the more value we would receive, up to 175 percent of the targeted award. The worse we did, the less we'd earn.

Our timing could not have been better. AMR's stock price rocketed past most of its competitors and the group of airlines shrunk as carriers filed for bankruptcy during the three-year measurement periods. The result: Beginning in 2006, top executives and other managers were entitled to receive payouts that ranged as high as 175 percent of the original award. The total payout to management exceeded three hundred million dollars.

We knew this was a good news/bad news story. It was great news for executives who would finally receive the "variable" portion of their compensation package approved by the board years earlier. To the board's credit, the plan worked exactly as designed. As the company's financial fortunes improved, measured by the performance of our stock price against the performance of other carriers' stock prices, executives received payouts. Likewise, if the stock had underperformed its competitors, executives would receive nothing.

But the bad news part of the story had all the makings of a really bad story. As we realized that executives would be entitled to huge payouts, Arpey and Brundage met with labor leaders to gauge their reaction to the upcoming stock payments.

Privately, union leadership acknowledged the efficacy of the executive compensation plan and understood the need to pay management. Publicly, it was another story. Labor leaders refused to support Arpey.

Instead, they elected to take the politically expedient path, one that played well to the rank and file, but created severe acrimony toward management. It was not enough to simply lodge their unhappiness with the payments. The Allied Pilots Association ("APA") decided to make the issue a *cause célèbre*. In their mind, management was once again hiding the ball and enriching themselves at the expense of rank and file employees. Arpey, like Carty, couldn't be trusted. It became a referendum on Arpey's trust-based "Pull Together, Win Together" tenet of the Turnaround Plan.

Long before the PUP payments were set to vest, the senior executives engaged in lengthy discussions and debates inside Arpey's conference room about how to handle the proposed payments. During one of those debates, someone at the table came up with the bright idea to just cancel the contracts and not make the payments at all.

Whenever a legal question arose, I was accustomed to all eyes immediately turning in my direction for some easy yes or no answer. Business people, even the most sophisticated, seem to think that lawyers can spit out legal advice and conclusions on command, no matter how complicated the issue.

I reminded the group that the Performance Unit Plan was a written contract signed by both the company and several hundred individual employees. Beyond that, I told the group I needed to review the contracts and the law before I could provide an answer.

When the meeting ended, I called Ken Wimberly and asked him to review the PUP contract and head down to my office to talk about it. He and I had worked together for many years and he was then vice president and corporate secretary. Ken, who took the job in 2005 when Chuck MarLett retired, was a walking encyclopedia of corporate governance procedures and SEC rules and regulations. I came to rely heavily on his judgment and I valued his legal opinion.

Ken walked into my office and I asked him what he thought. "So, Ken, what do you think? Can we cancel these contracts?"

Wimberly, always careful and deliberate, paused before responding. "Would we seriously consider not making the performance payments?"

"Ken, that's not the question. I know it would be a total shit storm, but can we cancel them if we decide to?"

"Technically, yes," he said. "There is a provision that gives the board the right to terminate the plan at any time, but I don't think it's enforceable."

This time it was my turn to pause before responding.

"I agree. Besides, some employees would probably end up suing us to enforce the contract. Then where would we be?"

"That's right," he responded. "The whole thing would be a mess. Back to my question. Are we really thinking about doing this?"

"I doubt it, but we are in one hell of a difficult situation with labor."

At another debate centered on the 2007 PUP payment, Arpey told the executive officers that he had decided to forgo 100 percent of the payment due him. He made this decision in spite of the fact that he didn't receive a PUP payment in 2006 because he refused to accept the stock awards granted to him by the board in 2003. He reasoned that by refusing payment, he could provide "cover" for the rest of the management team and use his sacrifice to curry favor with labor. He desperately hoped to placate labor and build upon the trust he worked so hard to establish with employees.

Privately, I pleaded with Arpey to accept the payment. I reminded him of the pact we made when he accepted the job as CEO—we would always do the right thing and always tell the truth.

"Look, Gerard, if you don't take the payment, it's a tacit acknowledgment that we're doing something wrong. And you and I both know that's not true. Besides, you're leaving millions of dollars on the table."

"I know. And the rest of the team should take the payment," he said. "But as CEO I'm the one with my neck on the line and I just can't do it. I made a promise to employees and I'll lose all credibility if I accept the money."

"Right, and do I need to remind you that you didn't accept a pay increase when you took the CEO job? I get what you're doing, but it's a slippery slope. If you don't take the payment now, when can you take a payment?" I asked.

"It sets a terrible precedent going forward and sends the wrong message to labor—that they're in charge of executive comp," I added.

"In any case, it's just not going to work. Labor is still going to raise hell about the payments."

"Well, you may be right. But I don't know what else to do," Gerard said. "The stakes are too high and it might just work."

In the end, we retained the program and it paid out as promised. Despite my admonition, Arpey waived his right to receive any payments. Labor's reaction to the payments was awful even though Gerard's sacrifice cost him millions of dollars.

From labor's perspective, management had once again lied and cheated its way to untold riches. They believed that Arpey and the senior executive team had intentionally developed a compensation plan designed to line their pockets without sharing the spoils with other employees. In short, they believed they had been duped.

Ralph Hunter, APA president, summed up labor's frustration and outrage.

"It is absolute insanity to pay out seven-figure bonuses at a time when the company is suffering nine-figure losses, mired in eleven-figure debt, and seeking further help from its employees," Hunter told pilots in a 2006 message sent after the company informed the unions of the pending payouts.

The problem with Hunter's statement to pilots was his characterization of the payments as "bonuses." The awards to management were not bonuses. The payments were an important component of an executive's pay package, disclosed in annual public SEC filings and discussed with labor long before the payments were made.

Labor's anger may have been tempered had employees received payments under the profit-sharing plan. Unfortunately, the airline didn't do well enough financially to trigger profit-sharing payments (so nonmanagement employees received nothing), but the airline's stock price did well versus the competition, triggering the massive payouts to management.

It's easy to understand labor's anger and frustration. While they limped along with concessionary contracts, management received hundreds of millions of dollars in payments and labor received nothing under the profit-sharing plan. Despite extraordinary and repeated efforts by Arpey and the rest of the team to explain to our employees the rationale behind the payments, nothing we said made any difference. Even efforts to communicate our message to local and national media held little sway. No one was listening.

Consequently, some labor leaders worked hard to discredit management and disrupt the airline. While the vast majority of employees were dedicated, hardworking individuals, the tactics used by certain union officials proved ruthless and unrelenting. At the 2007 Annual Meeting of Shareholders one employee referred to Arpey and other executives as "arrogant, greedy, selfish, and heartless individuals." That statement was mild in comparison to what labor leaders, particularly the pilots, unleashed in the coming months and years.

Under the direction of new APA president Lloyd Hill, elected in 2007, the pilots initiated what is commonly referred to in labor union circles as a "corporate campaign." The campaign was designed to embarrass and harass management at every turn. By the time the campaign was in full swing, we were in contract talks with all three company unions. The campaign lodged by union leadership against management was aggressive and mean-spirited. Even for veterans of previous corporate campaigns, the degree of vitriol and bullying was astonishing.

The APA attacked management on two fronts. One attack focused on management's alleged failure to properly operate the airline. The other line of attack focused directly on Arpey and other members of the executive team.

On the operational front, the APA sought to garner public sentiment by questioning management's competence to run the airline. One of their favorite tactics entailed the use of billboard advertisements to advance the union's agenda. One billboard was strategically located in Euless, Texas, just a few miles from AA's headquarters and DFW Airport. Thousands of travelers and company employees drove past this billboard every day. The message criticized the airline for flight cancellations:

AA's top priority? Not you!
250,884
late & canceled flights in '07

The union's tactics grew more brazen as the campaign continued, with the billboard messages turning to personal attacks on management:

AA executive bonuses since 2006
$295,000,000...and counting

The union organized picket lines outside the offices of large corporate customers of the airline. Union members also picketed outside the home of one well-known board member, NFL great Roger Staubach.

Incredulously, Hill and two other national union officers sent a letter to Arpey in September 2007 that directly blamed management and company policies for an uptick in suicide rates among the pilot workforce. The letter read in part:

Now that you have decided to start persecuting the most defenseless pilots in the group, disabled pilots with mental/ nervous disorders, we are seeing unprecedented suicide rates and pilots deserting their families. One pilot caught in this drive to reduce costs was forced to come off his medications to try to get his medical back. His reaction to this cessation of treatment was to leave his wife and children behind; we are trying reel him in before *he* kills himself.

The letter went on, "Enjoy your blood money and your union-busting meetings. We'll see you in court, in the newspapers and on the picket line."

On occasion, management unintentionally fanned the flames of discontent. My good friend and colleague, Jeff Brundage, made two statements to the media that created a furor among employees. The first was a statement he made to a Bloomberg reporter when questioned about American's labor costs, which at that time were the highest in the airline industry. Brundage said labor costs were "a big brick in our backpack to being competitive in the industry." That comment led to Brundage receiving the delivery of many bricks, compliments of employees. Separately, he once told a *Fort Worth Star-Telegram* reporter who asked about disgruntled pilots: "If they want to make what executives make, then they need to become executives."

We endured the corporate campaign leveled by labor leaders against management and did our best to ignore the rhetoric. But it was now 2008 and the modest financial success of 2006 and 2007 quickly gave way to a rapidly deteriorating economic outlook, along with labor costs that were at the top of the industry, two issues that promised big trouble for the airline. Despite these headwinds, labor's demands continued to escalate as the divide between management and labor grew ever larger.

During the many years of labor and management discontent, we had to deal with another controversy, one that had bedeviled American for decades—what to do about air service from Dallas's Love Field airport.

CHAPTER 6

LOVE IS A FOUR-LETTER WORD

B anquet tables were lined up end to end in the middle of the room. It was late spring 2006 and the setting was the Omni Mandalay, a hotel located approximately twenty minutes from DFW Airport. About twenty people in starched shirts and stiff business suits sat staring at one another across the width of the tables. But these were not typical conference room-style fixtures. These were hotel luncheon tables, dressed up with white linens. Consequently, they were narrow and gave the uneasy feeling of intimacy. Given the far-reaching consequences of the deal being negotiated, the participants needed more, not less, breathing room.

My senses told me something was amiss. I sniffed the air like an English setter on the lookout for birds hiding in the bush. I quickly realized what it was—the telltale sign of burning tobacco. Someone was smoking. I turned my head and looked up and down the length of the tables to locate the source of the offending smell. Confident that the smoke wafting through the room bothered others, I waited to see if anyone would ask the guilty party to douse the cigarette. I looked in the direction of Dallas Mayor Laura Miller. She gave a knowing glance, as if to say, "Leave it alone; let it pass." I nodded my head and tried not to breathe too deeply.

How I came to find myself in this hotel, on this day, negotiating an agreement among the cities of Dallas and Fort Worth, Southwest Airlines, American Airlines, and Dallas/Fort Worth International Airport, concerning the future of Dallas's oldest airport, Love Field, is a story that began one hundred years earlier, not long after Orville and Wilbur Wright successfully flew the first motor powered airplane in 1903.

The U.S. Army officially opened Love Field, located in Dallas, on October 19, 1917, some six months after the United States entered World War I. In 1927, the city of Dallas bought the airfield from the U.S. government. Similarly, Fort Worth in 1925 purchased an airfield from the U.S. Army and named it Meacham Field.

As the nation's interest in aviation grew, the two cities occasionally discussed the need for the construction of a single airport to serve the growing populace. While Dallas and Fort Worth are located just thirty-five miles from one another, "Big D" and "Cowtown" could never agree on the location of a centralized airport.

In the 1930s, Fort Worth and Dallas were cooperating on a proposed airport located between the cities until Dallas pulled out of the project, supposedly because the terminal was closer to and oriented toward Fort Worth. In 1953, Fort Worth purchased land and built an airport called Amon Carter Field, later renamed Greater Southwest International Airport, with Dallas declining to participate. (The American Airlines headquarters building constructed in the 1980s sits alongside of what was then the runway of Greater Southwest airport.)

Instead of supporting Greater Southwest, Dallas decided to replace its old Love Field terminal with a larger and more modern facility. The new terminal and gates opened in 1958. As time went on, air traffic migrated to Love Field, leaving Fort Worth's airport as the ugly stepchild. Eventually, most airlines abandoned Greater Southwest in favor of Love Field.

In 1964, the Civil Aeronautics Board (CAB), a longtime referee between the cities, finally got fed up. In 1964, it directed the cities to develop a plan for a regional airport that would serve the needs of the entire region. In those days, the CAB regulated most everything having to do with airlines, including airline routes and airfares. The CAB's order gave the cities exactly 180 days to come up with a proposal. With a deadline looming, Dallas and Fort Worth leaders overcame their historic animosity and selected a location for a new airport. Ironically, the site they selected was located just a few miles from Greater Southwest. Eventually, this site would be developed into one of the world's largest airports, to be known as Dallas/Fort Worth Regional Airport.

In 1968, Dallas and Fort Worth adopted bond ordinances that spelled out how the new airport would be financed. Those ordinances provided that all commercial airline service would relocate to the new Dallas/Fort Worth Regional Airport. All airlines then operating at Love Field and Greater Southwest signed agreements that contractually obligated them to move to the new airport when it opened.

But there was a fly in the ointment. One airline wasn't a party to the bond ordinances. The airline in question, Southwest Airlines, wasn't even authorized to operate as an air carrier in 1968. The airline, then called "Air Southwest," was the brainchild of San Antonio businessman Rollin King and attorney Herbert Kelleher. They dreamed up the idea for an airline that would provide intrastate service between Texas cities. The new airline made its first commercial flight on June 18, 1971.

In early 1971, airline veteran Lamar Muse joined the company as its chief executive officer. He soon made an announcement that had a profound effect on the future of North Texas aviation. He informed the CAB and the leaders of Dallas and Fort Worth that Southwest Airlines would not move to DFW Airport when it opened. He said that Love Field's convenient location, just six miles from downtown Dallas, suited Southwest's plans much better than an airport located in the distant suburbs.

The announcement was a bombshell that threatened to blow up the hard-won cooperation between Fort Worth and Dallas. The decision angered everyone. It angered the Dallas and Fort Worth city councils, it angered the buyers of the airport bonds (sold on the promise that there would be no commercial airline service at Love

Field), and it angered the airlines that had signed agreements to serve the new airport. With lots of angry constituents, there was no shortage of plaintiffs for the litigation that ensued.

As the litigation progressed in a variety of courtrooms, judges consistently agreed with the arguments advanced by Southwest. The upstart airline had not signed any legal agreement requiring it to move to the new airport, and was not bound by the covenants contained in the bond ordinances. The easiest and most expedient solution to the problem would have been to decommission Love Field and bulldoze it to the ground. But Dallas city leaders had no appetite to close Love Field outright. Dallas wanted to retain the valuable general aviation and aviation-related businesses at the airport.

The new Dallas/Fort Worth Regional Airport opened to great fanfare in January 1974. Southwest remained true to its convictions and was not part of the celebration. Instead, Southwest continued to grow its presence at Love Field, offering flights to cities throughout the State of Texas. As an intrastate carrier, Southwest didn't answer to the CAB, which regulated interstate service. But, the Dallas carrier also couldn't stray over the borders of Texas into different states.

Then, in 1978, Congress passed legislation to deregulate the airline industry and get rid of the CAB. Airlines were no longer forced to receive government approval before entering a new market.

Deregulation opened the door for Southwest to launch interstate service. The first destination selected by Southwest was New Orleans. Service to the Big Easy began in 1979 and immediately stirred up a new wave of resentment over Southwest's continued presence at Love Field.

Fort Worth had had enough. It turned to Congressman Jim Wright of Fort Worth for help. Congressman Wright was a legend in Texas politics and a powerful Democratic member of Congress. He represented the 12th Congressional District of Texas for thirty-four years and served as speaker of the House of Representatives from 1987 to 1989, before resigning on May 31, 1989, in the wake of an ethics scandal. Congressman Wright introduced legislation to bar all interstate flights out of Love Field. After much haggling, Congress passed a compromise that President Jimmy Carter signed into law in February 1980. The compromise, known as the Wright Amendment, was the subject of scorn and ridicule from the moment it became law.

The Wright Amendment limited commercial jet service from Love Field to airports in Texas and the four states contiguous to Texas—New Mexico, Oklahoma, Arkansas, and Louisiana. Aircraft with fifty-six seats or fewer (known as the commuter exception) were not covered by the limitation. This meant that airlines could fly commuter aircraft wherever they wanted out of Love Field. The law also barred carriers from selling tickets from Love Field to airports beyond the Wright Amendment perimeter.

For example, Southwest could not sell a passenger a ticket to fly from Dallas to Chicago, even with a stop in Oklahoma City. If someone wanted to fly Dallas-Chicago via Oklahoma City, that traveler had to first purchase a Dallas-Oklahoma City ticket, then purchase a separate ticket from Oklahoma City to Chicago. If the traveler had checked luggage, he or she had to go to baggage claim in Oklahoma City, pick up the luggage, carry it back to the ticket counter, and then recheck the luggage to Chicago.

Southwest hated the Wright Amendment because it severely limited its operations out of Love Field. Likewise, Fort Worth and the airlines serving DFW were angry because the Wright Amendment gave Southwest an even larger footprint at Love Field and allowed them to compete directly with DFW Airport.

The Wright Amendment was supposed to resolve, once and for all, the issue of airline service out of Love Field. In fact, Herb Kelleher, longtime chairman and CEO of Southwest, often declared that his airline was "passionately neutral" about the Wright Amendment, meaning he could live with it and would not seek to expand the service restrictions.

Over the years, the Wright Amendment withstood a variety of legal challenges in federal court. But, a number of constituencies remained unhappy about the law and were constantly searching for ways to modify it or repeal it completely. In 1997, Richard Shelby, a

Republican senator from Alabama, managed to make a dent in the law. He convinced Congress to add the states of Alabama, Kansas, and Mississippi (all represented by powerful U.S. senators) to the four-state perimeter rule. The change to the law became known as the "Shelby amendment." In 2005, one other state, Missouri, was added to the list, bringing the total to nine states (including Texas) that could be served out of Love Field.

In the late 1990s, Allan McArtor, former head of the Federal Aviation Administration, developed a novel approach to skirt the service restrictions at Love Field. He acquired old McDonnell Douglas DC-9s, removed a bunch of seats, and reconfigured the aircraft to stay within the fifty-six-seat commuter carrier exception. McArtor called his invention Legend Airlines. The seating configuration was essentially an all first-class cabin, with fine meals and generous amounts of elbowroom. Since his aircraft only had 56 seats, the airline could fly wherever it wished out of Love Field.

American didn't think McArtor's business plan had a chance in hell of working, but there was no way we were going to sit back and watch Legend steal any of our high-dollar clientele. We hatched an aggressive, yet costly, response. American took several of its one hundred-seat Fokker aircraft and reconfigured them to fifty-six seats. This gave us the ability to compete head-to-head with Legend at Love Field.

Legend launched service in April 2000 to Las Vegas, Los Angeles, and Washington, D.C., with flights to New York's LaGuardia Airport added in September. As predicted, the fledgling airline simply could not attract a sufficient revenue stream to offset its start-up and operating costs. Legend went belly up by the end of the year and became nothing more than an asterisk in the history of airline service at Love Field. American's Fokker flights didn't fare much better than Legend and we shut down our Love Field operation in 2001. I don't know if our competing service caused Legend's efforts to collapse. I do know that our Fokker service lost money, but I believe that Legend would have gone down in flames regardless of our competing service.

Life soon returned to normal at Love Field, but only for a few years. Herb Kelleher stepped down as CEO of Southwest Airlines in 2001. Jim Parker held the job for three years before CFO Gary Kelly took over in July 2004. It didn't take long for Kelly to distance himself from Kelleher's long-held "passionately neutral" stance over the Wright Amendment. In November of that same year, he announced that Southwest would push for a total repeal of the Wright Amendment.

Inside the headquarters at American Airlines, we were livid over Southwest's abandonment of its Switzerland-like position regarding the future of Love Field. To our way of thinking, Southwest got a free pass when it was allowed to continue operations at Love Field when DFW opened in 1974, and now it was rubbing salt in the wound with its effort to scuttle the Wright Amendment.

Kelly's declaration kicked the hornet's nest and set into motion a battle that waged throughout 2005 and well into 2006. American immediately launched an all-out ground assault to defeat Southwest's attack on the Wright Amendment. We directed our efforts at multiple constituencies, including those in Congress and local officials in Dallas and Fort Worth. On Capitol Hill, Will Ris, our government affairs guru in Washington, immediately geared up his substantial cadre of lobbyists and blanketed the halls of Congress.

Ris is a legend among airline lobbyists. In 1996, Crandall convinced Ris to leave the Wexler Group, a Washington, D.C.-based public relations firm. Ris served as American's top government affairs liaison for nearly twenty years before retiring at the end of 2015. He was universally liked and respected by members of Congress, in no small part due to his backhanded sense of humor.

Will's message was straightforward—a deal is a deal and no one has the right to mess with an arrangement that was agreed to and relied upon by all interested parties for the last twenty-five years.

We put forth a similar argument with local officials, particularly members of the Dallas City Council and the Fort Worth City Council. Not surprisingly, we received strong backing from Fort Worth officials and a slightly tepid reception from elected officials in Dallas.

By contrast, American had a difficult time attracting public support for its position. Not many people cared to hear about what happened twenty-five years earlier when the Wright Amendment was enacted. Most people considered Love Field convenient if they lived in Dallas, and they viewed the restrictions as silly and out of date. What sense did it make to have an airport that could only provide nonstop service in Texas and eight other states, and why in the world would a law force passengers to purchase two separate tickets and recheck their luggage on connecting flights? Other than a handful of citizens concerned about noise and congestion surrounding Love Field, abandoning the restrictions at the Dallas airport made a lot of sense to most people.

Not long after Love Field once again became a hot topic, Dallas Mayor Laura Miller and Fort Worth Mayor Mike Moncrief drove to American's headquarters to meet with Gerard Arpey. Arpey wanted reinforcements and he dragged me into the meeting with him. Mayor Miller assumed the role of spokesperson. I had never met her before that day, but we would soon end up spending a lot of time together over the next eighteen months. Laura Miller is impressive. She is smart, works hard, and is a strong advocate. When it suits her, she can also be incredibly charming.

Mayor Miller told us that the cities hoped to broker a deal that both American and Southwest could live with. She asked if there was any room for compromise in American's "a deal is a deal" mantra. Arpey's response was short and to the point—no way would we agree to any change in the Wright Amendment. Period. Mayor Miller was not accustomed to taking no for an answer and tried again to persuade Arpey to offer something, anything, that she could bring back to Southwest. Arpey didn't budge and the mayors left his office empty-handed.

Shortly after meeting with the two mayors, Arpey enlisted the assistance of NFL legend Roger Staubach. He was a member of American's board and anxious to help in any way he could. Together, they formulated a plan to meet with Kay Bailey Hutchison, the influential senior U.S. senator from Texas, so they could tell her in no uncertain terms that American would not agree to any changes to the Wright Amendment.

Arpey and Staubach met Senator Hutchison for a private lunch at Café Pacific in Highland Park, an exclusive suburb of Dallas. The meeting did not go as planned. Arpey and Staubach opened the meeting and launched into a well-rehearsed explanation about the righteousness of American's position. They didn't get very far before Senator Hutchison told them she had heard quite enough. She then hit the pair right between the eyes with her own "come to Jesus" missive. In a tone reminiscent of a rant from a high school football coach, she told Arpey and Staubach that American needed to start playing ball and quickly figure out a sensible solution to the Love Field problem. If American didn't get on board, she warned, the whole thing was going to blow up in American's face and Congress would soon abolish Love Field restrictions altogether.

According to Arpey, lunch didn't taste so good following Hutchison's lecture, but he and Staubach understood the senator loud and clear. From that day forward, while American advanced its "no way in hell" message to external constituencies, we quietly signaled to Mayor Miller a willingness to consider alternatives.

But a compromise proved difficult to craft. We had a genuine concern that Love Field, with plenty of vacant terminal and gate space, could expand greatly in size and scope, enabling it to compete head-to-head with DFW Airport. Such a scenario would allow Southwest to lure large numbers of American's valued customers to the more convenient downtown airport, something we could not tolerate unless we found a way to limit the potential loss.

What followed was North Texas's version of high stakes peace negotiations. Even though the gulf between American and Southwest was huge, Mayor Miller plowed headlong into the fray. Like Henry Kissinger, Miller employed her own version of shuttle diplomacy in an effort to find common ground between the two warring airlines.

After countless meetings and phone calls with officials from DFW and Love Field, the airlines, congressional leaders, and countless other groups that had a vested interest in the outcome, the mayor's shuttle diplomacy began to bear fruit. The seeds of a possible deal were rooted in the elimination of all air service restrictions at Love Field, a concept that American originally said it would never entertain. The underlying question was one of timing. When would the air service restrictions be lifted—one year, five years, or ten years down the road? And what of the restrictions on through ticketing and checked luggage? An even more pressing question figured into the calculus—what was in it for American Airlines?

If we agreed to support a modification to the Wright Amendment, it was essential that new constraints be implemented that addressed the overall size and utilization of the airport. Without sensible limitations to counterbalance the newfound liberalization of air service, the deal made no sense for American.

One constraint at the top of our list focused on limiting the total amount of flight activity at the airport. We insisted that there be a hard cap on the number of gates at Love Field. With so much vacant space at the airport, we were afraid that Southwest or another airline would construct a new multi-gate facility unless we put a stake in the ground that limited future growth.

We also insisted that Love Field be restricted to domestic air service only, with all international flights being accommodated out of DFW Airport. There was good precedent to bolster our position. International flights require federal customs and immigration personnel and the government generally limits its staffing to one airport in a geographic region.

Back and forth negotiations continued without respite. Mayor Miller had her heels directly on the necks of the two airlines as she pressured us to make a deal. She was relentless, telephoning at all hours to hammer out the latest twist or turn in the negotiations. The mayor called me frequently at home, often late at night. Before I would even answer the phone, my wife would occasionally comment, "Please tell the Mayor hello for me."

While I was dealing with Mayor Miller, Will Ris continued to press American's case on Capitol Hill, frequently calling on Arpey to join him in Washington. It became abundantly clear that the future of Love Field was not just a local issue. It was much more of a national issue with implications far beyond North Texas. Not only were Arpey and Kelleher called to testify in Congress about the Love Field problem, it was also an issue that came to the attention of a fellow Texan, President George W. Bush.

For many years, American Airlines was a sponsor of an annual performance at the Ford Theatre in Washington, D.C. During the midst of the Love Field controversy, Arpey and his wife attended one of the performances and were seated next to the president and First Lady Laura Bush. During the intermission, the president inquired about Love Field, and Arpey did his best to give the president a concise summary of the difficult problems associated with the expansion of flights out of the Dallas airport. President Bush then asked Arpey a pointed question about Southwest's chairman: "Do you trust the guy?" Gerard thought carefully before responding. "Yes, Mr. President, I know Mr. Kelleher quite well...I do trust him."

As the discussions over the future of the Wright Amendment progressed, the parties coalesced around a conceptual framework of a deal. There were four principal elements: (1) flight restrictions at Love Field would expire in eight years; (2) through ticketing and baggage restrictions would be lifted immediately; (3) the maximum size of the airport would be limited to twenty gates (with Southwest being allocated fifteen gates and increasing to sixteen, American getting three gates but decreasing to two, and regional carrier ExpressJet Airlines receiving the last two gates); and (4) flights originating out of Love Field would be limited to domestic service only.

The basic elements of the arrangement were acceptable to American, but there remained an issue that worried us. We were concerned that Southwest, always sly as a fox, would find a way to "have its cake at Love Field and eat it at DFW." As structured, Southwest would get the prize it so desperately wanted—the elimination of flight restrictions at Love Field. But it came with a price—a twenty-gate cap. With growth at the airfield limited by the cap, how and where would Southwest grow in the future?

The choice was obvious—Dallas/Fort Worth International Airport. It seemed fundamentally unfair for Southwest to control 80 percent (eventually growing to 90 percent) of the gates at Love Field, then expand its footprint by initiating service at DFW. Over the years, whenever the media or consumer groups derided the Wright Amendment's service restrictions as arcane or anticompetitive, we were quick to point out that Southwest was free to commence service at DFW at any time it desired. In fact, we encouraged Southwest to compete head-to-head with American at DFW Airport.

We crafted a unique solution to the problem. We proposed that if Southwest initiated passenger service at any airport within an 80-mile radius of Love Field (the radius was meant to cover the unlikely event that a surrounding city opened a commercial airport), it would be required to relinquish one gate at Love Field for every gate it utilized at the other airport, up to a maximum of eight gates. The obligation to relinquish gates would extend until the year 2025. To level the playing field, a similar obligation applied to American (up to one and one half gates) if we initiated passenger service at an airport other than DFW or Love Field that was located within the eighty-mile radius.

Southwest hated the proposal, and others cried that the provision smacked of anticompetitive behavior. We disagreed and argued that the proposal was actually pro-competitive. If Southwest wanted to compete at DFW (which American welcomed), then it should be required to loosen its stranglehold on Love Field and allow others the opportunity to compete.

As the parties moved closer to achieving a final resolution to the Wright Amendment, one additional concern nagged at Arpey. It was the same concern he directed to me and Will Ris time and again.

Even though Will's main office was in Washington, he would typically spend the early part of each week at our DFW headquarters. On one such occasion, Gerard summoned me and Will to his office. "If we agree to this deal," he asked, "how can you guarantee that it will never be changed? What if someone decides they want a different deal ten years from now?"

Arpey was right to be concerned. When the Wright Amendment was enacted in 1980, the legislation was supposed to put all Love Field issues to rest, yet here we were fighting about the same issues again. What's more, Senator Shelby convinced Congress to modify the Wright Amendment in 1997, so what would prevent the same thing from happening again? Will and I both knew we had to convince Arpey that the deal was rock solid or he wouldn't support it.

"Well," Gerard asked, looking at me and Will, "what's different this time around?"

Will spoke up first. "The Wright and Shelby amendments were simple legislative fixes to the problem," he told Gerard. "This time there will be a binding contract signed by five parties, plus new legislation. The only way to change anything in the future is to convince all five parties to modify the contract *and* to convince Congress to amend the law."

Earlier, I had discussed the issue at length with Mike Powell, a litigator and senior partner at Locke Lord in Dallas. Powell was an expert on Love Field. He had been advising us about the Wright Amendment for many years and was directly involved in the current negotiations. I trusted his advice and was confident of the position Will advanced to Arpey.

"I sure hope you're right about this," Gerard said.

"Trust us, Gerard, it will work," I replied.

With a conceptual understanding agreed to by the five parties, Ris, along with his counterparts at Southwest and DFW Airport, had to convince both houses of Congress to support the proposed plan and pass legislation modifying the Wright Amendment. While most members of Congress didn't favor air service restrictions at Love Field (many of whom were enamored with Southwest's low-cost model), nevertheless it was a challenge to convince Congress to repeal the Wright Amendment and enact a series of new restrictions in its place.

Congressional leaders representing the Dallas-Fort Worth region worked in a collaborative and bipartisan manner to craft legislation and garner support from both Democrats and Republicans. And no one in Congress was more instrumental than Senator Kay Bailey Hutchison in fashioning a winning legislative strategy.

While work continued in Washington, D.C., on the legislative front, the five parties to the agreement, along with their attorneys, agreed to a face-to-face meeting at the Omni Mandalay, to iron out the remaining issues. From American's perspective, we had one shot to get this right and couldn't afford to leave a loophole for Southwest to jump through, just as it had done thirty-five years earlier when Southwest initiated service at Love Field. We needed an additional set of eyes and ears at the meeting, so Gerard asked Dan Garton, who was then our executive vice president of marketing, to join me at the negotiating table.

This brings me back to the smoke-filled room with the power-brokers of North Texas. Dan and I arrived at the hotel and walked into the meeting room. This had been a legally complex set of negotiations and a difficult political problem. The dispute over air travel in the region was decades long and maybe with some luck and another difficult meeting, the issue would finally be put to bed.

There were representatives of each of the five parties, plus their attorneys, milling about. No one was formally in charge of the meeting, but that duty, by default, fell to Kevin Cox, the chief operating officer at DFW Airport. Weeks earlier, he had accepted the task of preparing and reducing to writing the conceptual framework of the agreement. With five sets of attorneys providing redline changes each time he circulated a draft for comment, Cox became the ring-leader of a bizarre circus.

Once underway, the parties addressed a long list of questions and concerns. It seemed that danger lurked behind most every part of the agreement. The twenty-gate cap, a seemingly unambiguous element of the transaction, was not as simple as it first appeared. We had dissected the twenty-gate cap from all angles but remained concerned that Southwest would try to find a way around the limit.

What if Southwest parked two aircraft on a single gate by using two jet bridges? Could that be considered one gate, or is it now two gates? Could Southwest park aircraft at a remote hardstand on the airfield and bus passengers to the terminal and not violate the twenty-gate cap? The answer from American was a resounding no. We tightened the language of the agreement to make it crystal clear that Southwest could not subdivide a gate and could not use hardstands on the ramp.

We also demanded strict assurances that the unused gate facilities at the airport would be demolished without delay. The then-existing Love Field master plan called for thirty-two gates at the airport and there was ample room to accommodate that number of gates. Until a wrecking ball reduced the excess facilities to rubble, there was plenty of opportunity for Southwest-style mischief. We wouldn't sleep well until there was absolute certainty that there would never be more than twenty gates at Love Field. To accomplish this, we demanded that the city of Dallas spend between one hundred and fifty million dollars and two hundred million dollars to redevelop and modernize Love Field.

While we sat in the hotel conference room and pounded out the details of the agreement, I soon found the source of the annoying cigarette smoke wafting through the room. The guilty party was Southwest's chairman and former CEO Herb Kelleher. No one dared remind him that the hotel was a nonsmoking facility. One could say that no place was a nonsmoking zone for Herb, who would light up, on occasion, in elevators or in special rooms set aside by his favorite restauranteurs. I decided that a dry-cleaning bill was a small price to pay if we could put air service at Love Field in the rearview mirror once and for all.

Following the day-long hotel confab, the remaining pieces of the deal soon fell into place. The five parties to the agreement—the cities of Dallas and Fort Worth, Dallas/Fort Worth International Airport, Southwest Airlines, and American Airlines—signed the final contract on July 11, 2006. Not long after, Congress enacted conforming legislation that adopted the terms of the agreement. President George W. Bush signed the legislation, and it went into effect on October 13, 2006.

Eight years later, on October 13, 2014, at 6:40 a.m., the first Southwest Airlines flight departed Love Field en route to Denver. With that flight, the thirty-four-year old Wright Amendment perimeter rule was officially relegated to the history books.

As I write this, the promise Will Ris and I made to Gerard Arpey in 2006 remains intact. No one, including Southwest, has attempted to modify the "final" resolution reached by the parties. For now, I am pleased. Only time will tell if our promise will last forever.

CHAPTER 7

FLIGHT 587

Events at large companies like American Airlines do not unfold in an orderly fashion. They reveal themselves in random, unstructured, and chaotic ways. The controversy surrounding Love Field was a commercial dispute, one that developed over a long number of years. Other events strike without warning.

On Sunday, November 11, 2001, Captain Ed States, age forty-two, enjoyed a relaxing day with his family at their two-story home in Plainsboro, New Jersey. Plainsboro is a small town outside of Princeton. Like most every Sunday, States attended church in the morning. When he returned home he watched a bit of television. He and his wife, Mary Alden, were the parents of two young boys, which accounted for the Cub Scouts meeting that Ed went to later in the day. That night, he went to bed around 10 p.m., knowing he had to wake up early the next morning.

Captain States joined American Airlines in July 1985. He was a military pilot by training, and by 2001 had accumulated over eight thousand hours of flying time. On the morning of November 12, States woke up at approximately 4:15 and left his home forty-five minutes later for the drive to New York's John F. Kennedy International Airport (JFK), about sixty miles from Plainsboro. Records indicate that he checked in for Flight 587 at approximately 6:14 a.m.

First Officer Sten Molin, age thirty-four, was born in the Queens area of New York. By the time he was eighteen years old, he dreamed of flying airplanes. Molin asked his father, a former commercial airline pilot, to teach him. According to his father, Sten was a quick learner and a skilled pilot.

Like Captain States, Molin engaged in a variety of leisurely activities on November 11. He helped a friend winterize her sailboat, then went out for lunch. That evening, he had dinner at home with friends. Molin set his alarm clock for 5:30 a.m. When he woke up, he traveled to JFK and checked in for Flight 587 at approximately 6:30 a.m.

Flight 587 was scheduled to depart JFK for Santo Domingo, Dominican Republic, early Monday morning, November 12, 2001. The thirteen-year-old aircraft was an Airbus A300, one of only thirty-five Airbus aircraft in American's fleet. It was a full flight with 251 passengers on board, including five lap children, plus nine crew members. Sixty-eight of the passengers were citizens of the Dominican Republic and many more were of Dominican descent. Some were going home to visit relatives. One was a sixty-nine-year-old widow, with twelve surviving children. Another was a sailor headed home to see his three sons, including a baby boy the Navy petty officer had last seen eleven days after the baby's birth. In a number of cases, two or more members of the same family were traveling together. As passengers completed the boarding process, a twenty-four-year-old law student and his forty-eight-year-old mother were at home in Belle Harbor, New York, a small affluent town located just twelve miles from JFK airport. Three of their neighbors were also at home going about their morning routine.

The weather conditions were perfect for flying that morning, with a temperature of 42 degrees and partly cloudy skies. After the passengers were seated and the pilots completed their pre-departure checks, the aircraft received clearance from the tower to push back from the gate. It was 8:59 a.m.

A few minutes later, Captain States and First Officer Molin taxied the aircraft to Runway 31L. States made the decision to have Molin "fly" the aircraft that morning and told him, "Your leg, you check the rudders." Molin then tested the operation of the right rudder, followed by the left rudder. When he was finished, Molin responded to Captain States, "Rudders check."

About this same time, the tower cleared Japan Airlines Flight 47 (JAL) for takeoff. The JAL aircraft was a Boeing 747 and was scheduled to depart on the same runway as American 587. The controller instructed the American pilots to depart after JAL. Because the Japan Airlines aircraft was a jumbo jet, the tower cautioned States and Molin about the possibility of encountering wake turbulence after takeoff.

An Airbus A300 is no lightweight itself. Empty, it weighs just under two hundred thousand pounds, more than twice the weight of the Boeing 737s or Airbus A321s that now dominate American's single-aisle fleet. But the Boeing 747, like the one JAL was flying, was much larger, more than double the weight of the Airbus A300. Consequently, American's A300 needed to be a safe distance behind the JAL aircraft so the Airbus wouldn't be unduly rocked by the air disturbances stirred up from the 747.

Shortly after Flight 587 was cleared for takeoff, First Officer Molin asked Captain States, "You happy with that [separation] distance?" States replied, "We'll be all right once we get rollin'. He's supposed to be five miles by the time we're airborne, that's the idea."

The American Airbus lifted off runway 31L into the skies above New York City at 9:14 a.m. The aircraft climbed to 500 feet, turned left, and proceeded to an altitude of 1,300 feet. The flight controller then instructed the American pilots to climb to 13,000 feet. Twenty-four seconds later, Captain States said "clean machine." In aviation parlance, States's use of the term meant that the aircraft's landing gear, flaps, and slats were all retracted.

Just sixty-plus seconds later, the situation onboard Flight 587 quickly deteriorated. The aircraft, now at about 2,300 feet, encountered wake turbulence from the JAL aircraft. Captain States commented to Molin, "Little wake turbulence, huh?" Molin responded, "Yeah." Beginning at 9:15:51, the cockpit voice recorder (CVR) recorded the sound of "a thump, a click, and two thumps," all in quick succession over a period of a little more than one second.

Molin then called for "max power." By this time, his voice was strained.

"You all right?" Captain States asked.

"Yeah, I'm fine," Molin responded.

But things weren't fine. Just one second after Molin assured States that everything was OK, the captain yelled, "Hang onto it. Hang onto it." Molin responded, "Let's go for power please." Then, at 9:15:57, the CVR records the sounds of a loud thump and a snap.

The final twelve seconds of Flight 587 were chilling. At 9:16, Molin is heard saying, "holy [expletive]," followed by a stall warning and the first officer's words, "What the hell are we into...? We're stuck in it." The CVR ends with the final words from Captain States, "Get out of it, get out of it."

Flight 587 crashed into a neighborhood in Belle Harbor, New York. All 260 passengers and flight crew on board the aircraft were killed. In addition, five people from Belle Harbor, including the law student and his mother, perished and several homes in the area were destroyed or severely damaged.

It appeared that the vertical stabilizer—the tall tail fin at the back of the airplane, essential to controlling the airplane—had simply broken off. According to the report issued by the NTSB, the main attachment fitting of the vertical stabilizer fractured at 9:15:58 and the vertical stabilizer detached from the airplane immediately thereafter. The stabilizer and the aircraft's rudder were later found in Jamaica Bay. The aircraft's two engines separated during the last several seconds of flight and were found several blocks from the main wreckage.

News of the crash stunned CEO Don Carty and the entire American Airlines family. Only two months earlier, the airline suffered immense tragedy in the wake of the 9/11 terrorist attacks. It was almost inconceivable that tragedy had once again struck at the heart of the airline.

Carty's first thoughts turned immediately to the families of those killed in the crash. Without a moment's hesitation, he activated American's CARE team, an expert group of employees trained to respond in the event of an incident involving one of our aircraft.

Despite extraordinary air travel safety records, American and all commercial airlines understand the risks associated with air travel and are well prepared to respond in times of crisis.

As word of the crash quickly spread, speculation swirled about the cause of the accident. Given the close proximity to 9/11, news media immediately raised the possibility that the crash was another terrorist strike. Fearing the worst, New York Mayor Rudy Giuliani closed bridges and tunnels leading into the city. As Carty prepared to fly to New York, he received a phone call from Giuliani. The mayor was in a helicopter flying over Jamaica Bay and the site of the accident. Giuliani remarked to Carty that he could see the wing of the aircraft lying in the bay. Carty knew better. He corrected the mayor and told him that it was likely the rudder of the aircraft, not the wing. Shortly after that conversation, Carty flew to New York to hold a news conference to express his condolences to the family members of the deceased.

It didn't take long for accident investigators from the National Transportation Safety Board (NTSB) to reach a preliminary conclusion that the accident was the result of a massive mechanical malfunction, with no evidence pointing to a terrorist strike. NTSB Chairwoman Marion Blakey confirmed this view in a statement to the media: "All information we have currently is that this is an accident. All communications from the cockpit were normal up until the last few seconds before the crash. It points to no criminal activity."

All aviation disasters are horrific. Flight 587 was particularly difficult for American Airlines. The company suffered immense hardship as a result of the terrorist attacks of September 11, 2001. We lost twenty-three valued members of the American Airlines family and 167 passengers on the two aircraft that crashed into the World Trade Center and the Pentagon. Thousands more on the ground were killed. The company and its employees were in the early stages of recovering from the tragedy of 9/11 and remained in a tenuous state, both emotionally and financially. The losses sustained on November 12, 2001, compounded feelings of despair within an already fragile company.

As the leader of American Airlines, Don Carty carried the immense burden of holding the company together after the terrorist strikes of 9/11. It was a monumental task. With this latest disaster, Carty pondered the near impossible road ahead. "We've lost the company," he thought to himself. "We can't survive this latest tragedy." Miraculously, the company found a path forward.

In the months and years following the crash of Flight 587, families mourned the loss of loved ones. Inevitably, mourning turned to anger, compounded by unanswered questions about why Flight 587 suffered such catastrophic failure shortly after takeoff. Lawyers representing the families of the deceased filed lawsuits against American and Airbus seeking to understand what happened, and for monetary damages against the two companies. American Airlines responded to those lawsuits and assigned blame to Airbus, claiming that defects in the design of the rudder control system were the primary cause of the accident. Airbus countered, arguing that American was at fault, citing pilot error and First Officer Molin's excessive use of the rudder while flying through the wake turbulence of the recently departed JAL flight.

The NTSB conducted an exhaustive investigation of Flight 587 in an effort to determine the probable cause of the crash. The NTSB established eleven separate teams of experts to conduct the investigation. Both American and Airbus submitted written statements to the NTSB and the agency conducted a four-day public hearing in Washington, D.C., beginning October 29, 2002.

On October 26, 2004, the five-member NTSB issued its official Aircraft Accident Report. The findings of probable cause of the accident are found on page 160 of that report:

The National Transportation Safety Board determines that the probable cause of this accident was the in-flight separation of the vertical stabilizer as a result of the loads beyond ultimate design that were created by the first officer's unnecessary and excessive rudder pedal inputs. Contributing to these rudder pedal inputs were characteristics of the Airbus

A300-600 rudder system design and elements of the American Airlines Advanced Aircraft Maneuvering Program.

Two NTSB board members, Carol Carmody and Richard Healing, issued a separate statement regarding probable cause. These members disagreed with the order in which the contributing factors were listed in the report. According to Carmody and Healing, the draft NTSB report listed first the American Airlines Advanced Aircraft Maneuvering Program, followed by the Airbus rudder design. The final report reversed the order of these two findings.

A total of 374 wrongful death lawsuits were filed against American Airlines and Airbus by families of the passengers and those killed on the ground (frequently with multiple lawsuits filed in connection with a single fatality). The lawsuits were filed in several jurisdictions, but later consolidated in the Southern District of New York. The judge assigned to hear the cases was Judge Robert W. Sweet, a then eighty-one-year-old, Yale-educated jurist appointed to the court by President Jimmy Carter in 1978. Overseeing such a large number of wrongful death cases was a huge undertaking, with numerous procedural and substantive legal issues to be decided long before the cases would find their way to a jury.

Judge Sweet was soon faced with a critical question in the case— what body of law should govern the calculation of damage awards to families of deceased passengers? American, through its lawyers at Condon & Forsyth, a law firm specializing in aircraft accident litigation, along with the attorneys representing Airbus, teed up the question by filing a motion with Judge Sweet, arguing that New York state law should apply. Lawyers for the victims countered that the law of admiralty was the appropriate standard for damage awards.

The answer to the question had far-reaching economic consequences for the families. Under New York law, families were not entitled to damages for "loss of society." In other words, they could not be compensated for the loss of love, care, and companionship of their family members killed as a result of the crash. The opposite result held true under admiralty law. The application of admiralty law in aviation accidents that occur over water has been the subject of significant litigation over the years. Judge Sweet carefully considered the arguments on both sides of the question.

Ultimately, Judge Sweet ruled in favor of the plaintiffs. According to Chris Christensen at the Condon law firm, Judge Sweet reasoned that admiralty law applied to the case because the ferrying of people across an ocean to an island is a "function traditionally performed by waterborne vessels," such that the flight had a "significant relationship to traditional maritime activity."

Slowly, over a matter of years, American and Airbus resolved each of the wrongful death lawsuits in advance of trial. The final lawsuit was settled in 2009, eight years after the accident.

As American and Airbus worked to settle the wrongful death lawsuits with the victims' families, litigation between the two companies on the issue of fault continued without resolution. As the litigation moved forward, I kept Arpey and the executive team updated on developments. American and Airbus each blamed the other for the tragic events and neither party seemed willing to budge from their respective positions. Despite the strong convictions of both parties, neither company relished the idea of a protracted and public airing of the facts surrounding the accident.

In an effort to find common ground and avoid trial, we engaged in a series of mediated discussions in Judge Sweet's courtroom. Unlike other commercial disputes, I found these discussions painful. Each time I met with attorneys and representatives of Airbus, it was an instant reminder of the circumstances that brought us together. After several difficult meetings, American and Airbus reached a final resolution in June 2008. The terms of that settlement agreement remain confidential.

Like so many airline disasters, scores of innocent people died in the crash of Flight 587, and the accident shattered the lives of family members and friends of the deceased. For American, the accident tested the company's resilience. In the period of just two months, American had suffered two catastrophic events—the September 11 terrorist attacks and the loss of Flight 587. No other airline had ever experienced such devastation.

In the years following the accident, American pressed forward despite the odds. By the time the litigation between American and Airbus was resolved and the last of the victim lawsuits was settled, American was mired in a daily battle for survival in the midst of a worldwide financial collapse.

CHAPTER 8

RACE AGAINST TIME

The years between 2008 and 2011 were difficult ones for American Airlines. By 2008, we were mired in negotiations with our labor unions, and there was no light at the end of the tunnel. Labor was demanding new "supersized" contracts. Not only did they want us to restore what they lost in 2003, they wanted substantial wage increases, along with improved benefits and work rules. This, despite the fact that virtually every major competitor had restructured their labor contracts in bankruptcy, giving them an enormous cost advantage over American.

On top of our labor problems, the U.S. housing bubble began its well-documented crash, which quickly led to misery in worldwide financial markets. The resulting recession of 2008 (now referred to as the Great Recession) will be remembered as the worst economic downturn since the Great Depression of the 1930s. A financial crisis of this magnitude, combined with record high fuel prices, resulted in catastrophic results for the company. Between 2008 and 2011, American Airlines lost a total of 6.1 billion dollars. That equates to a loss of four million dollars every day. These kinds of bone-chilling financial results were not sustainable. We had to find a way out.

At the end of March 2007, Ed Brennan retired from the board after nearly twenty years of service to American Airlines. Not only did his departure create a vacancy on the board, it also left us without a lead director. The lead director is a position of great importance because that person serves as the spokesperson and direct intermediary between the executive team and the board of directors. Ed Brennan had vast experience in corporate governance and filled this role with aplomb. Given the many challenges facing the company, we needed Ed's replacement to have the same poise and experience.

It was no surprise that Gerard Arpey and the board turned to Armando Codina to fill Brennan's shoes as lead director. Codina was a self-made man in the truest sense of the word. He fled Cuba decades earlier with nothing but a strong work ethic, perseverance, intelligence, and a bucket of charisma. He built a real estate business worth hundreds of millions of dollars and became a highly sought-after board member of big-name companies like Merrill Lynch, General Motors, and Home Depot.

During Arpey's tenure as CEO, he came to rely upon Codina's sage advice and business acumen. Gerard knew that he could always count on Armando during difficult times. And the years leading up to 2011 were filled with difficulty.

At the beginning of each week, the senior executives gathered in Arpey's conference room for a planning and strategy session. These meetings were long and covered a wide spectrum of issues. They often turned tedious as we poured over the latest financial results, booking trends, aircraft refurbishment plans, FAA directives, labor issues, and legal matters. Lunch was a welcome break, but even it became monotonous. The menu didn't vary much. A cold sandwich or lukewarm pizza, all served on plastic plates, was standard fare. Not exactly the vision of a high-powered executive lunch.

Near the conclusion of the meeting, each senior officer would report on the latest events or issues in his or her department. Many of the officers made short work of their report, God bless them. Others used it as a vehicle to describe in excruciating detail obscure and seemingly mundane matters, quickly driving my colleagues and me into fits of boredom. There was one officer in particular who religiously droned on for what seemed like an eternity. Whenever it was his turn to speak, several of us on my end of the table started a betting pool, wagering on how long he would talk. The stakes were high. One dollar to get in the pool, and whoever came closest to guessing the total minutes of elapsed speaking time collected the winnings. It required a fair bit of cunning and skill to win consistently. While there is no official record to substantiate the claim, I am confident that I won the pool more often than anyone else.

One of the issues we discussed at great length in our planning meetings was the price of jet fuel. It was a main contributor to our wretched financial results.

For airlines, fuel is the lifeblood of the business. It is often the single largest operating expense.

In 2008, American and its regional partners operated more than 3,400 flights per day, every day of the year. Some flights are short, like DFW to Tyler, Texas, a 20-minute, 103-mile flight. Others are much longer. The Dallas to Hong Kong flight is over eight thousand miles—it is so long that passengers depart on a Monday morning, fly over the international dateline, and arrive on Tuesday afternoon, having been in the air for over seventeen hours. Wilbur and Orville would be astonished. What these flights have in common is that they all need fuel, lots of it.

In 2000, we paid 2.5 billion dollars for jet fuel. By 2008, the year the Great Recession hit, our fuel bill had jumped to a little over nine billion dollars. Consequently, our operating results went from marginally profitable in 2006 and 2007 to massively unprofitable in 2008 and afterward.

With our yearly losses continuing to climb, Tom Horton, who returned as CFO in 2006, along with Bev Goulet, our vice president and corporate treasurer, focused on building cash reserves to weather the financial storm. That meant borrowing money whenever and wherever we could. Goulet and her team examined every "stick of furniture" on the company's books to determine which assets could be leveraged for cash. Their efforts resulted in a myriad of highly complicated financings, including aircraft, aircraft engines, spare parts, our headquarters buildings, and intangible assets like frequent flyer miles.

One financing in particular stands out. In 2009, the treasury crew decided to use miles in our world-renowned frequent flyer program, AAdvantage, as security for a loan from our biggest partner, Citibank. For years, and continuing today, American and Citibank have been partners in a successful program whereby users of Citi credit cards earn AAdvantage miles for every purchase. In exchange, Citi pays American for each mile awarded. This arrangement, known in the industry as an "affinity" card program, reaps huge benefits to both parties by building an ever-expanding base of loyal customers.

The structure of the loan from Citi was simple on its face, yet the details were extraordinarily complex. Given the difficult nature of the transaction, we assembled a robust team of internal and external lawyers to put the deal together. Otto Grunow, AA's associate general counsel in charge of corporate transactions, headed up the internal legal team, and Jan Sharry, a senior partner at Haynes and Boone, a Dallas-based law firm, served as outside counsel. Otto and Jan are both experts in putting together complex corporate transactions.

Basically, Citi agreed to "prepurchase" AAdvantage miles from American. In essence, it was a "forward sale" of miles instead of the usual arrangement whereby Citi paid for miles after they were accrued. We were borrowing against the future—not something a company likes to do but we needed cash immediately.

The scale of the prepurchase was staggering—one billion dollars. Given American's rocky financial footing, Citi demanded, and received, assurances that its loan to American was secure and that it would be repaid over time even if American were forced into bankruptcy.

The effort to raise cash was enormously successful. By late 2011, American's cash reserves stood at 4.1 billion dollars. But amassing such a tidy sum of cash came with a big price tag. It was virtually all borrowed money—money that needed to be repaid. What's more, because we leveraged almost every asset on the books, we had virtually nothing to use as collateral for a DIP loan if we later needed one.

A DIP loan is "Debtor in Possession" financing arranged with bankers immediately before or after a bankruptcy filing. This kind of financing gives the debtor the cash needed to continue operating while the bankruptcy case makes its way through the court. Horton, Goulet, and I had lots of discussions about this issue, and we made sure that our board was fully aware that the effort to raise cash now was, by and large, a form of "Pre-DIP" financing and that nothing would be available as security in a bankruptcy scenario. Without assets for a DIP, insolvency was a genuine risk if we did not maintain a sufficient cash balance.

Monitoring our cash balance became an obsession. To make sure we never fell below the minimum cash required to survive a bankruptcy, Goulet's team developed a model designed to monitor cash requirements. The model plotted two lines on a graph. One line tracked a forecast of total available cash by month, and the second tracked something called the "Minimum Cash Threshold" or "MCT" for short. The line representing total cash needed to stay comfortably ahead of the line representing the MCT. If the lines crossed, we knew we were in real trouble.

The bad news on the financial front wasn't the only obstacle facing American. A host of frightening risks were spelled out in our SEC filings and read like a Stephen King novel—future terrorist attacks; overseas conflicts and war; political instability in foreign countries; infectious diseases like avian bird flu, SARS, H1N1, and Ebola; earthquakes and volcanic eruptions; and fuel shortages. The list seemed endless. To our chagrin, these risks were real, not imagined. We often joked that the only thing missing from the list were an infestation of locusts.

We never knew which among the parade of horribles might raise its head and unleash some new havoc on the airline. Life in the airline business was rife with challenges, making it difficult to remain upbeat. But, as Arpey said time and again to anyone who would listen, "We may be disappointed, but we are not discouraged."

As the airline battled one difficulty after another, I still had a legal department to run. With a large company like American, there was never a shortage of issues and challenges. One challenge in particular became a focal point of my tenure as general counsel—the hiring and advancement of diverse employees throughout the company. In addition, I spearheaded an effort to increase the number of diverse attorneys at the company, and to increase the use of diverse talent at law firms we hired to handle our legal business. Thanks to our HR department and attorneys who worked in the legal department, we advanced an agenda that emphasized diversity in the broadest sense of the word—race, sexual orientation, sexual identification, disability, religion, and national origin.

In 2004, American Airlines was one of the few Fortune 100 companies in the country that had a diversity committee as a standing committee of the board. For many years, the chair of the diversity committee was Earl Graves, a champion of minority advancement and a national spokesperson in the African-American community. When Graves retired from the board in 2008, Roger Staubach accepted the chairmanship of the committee.

American's foray into diversity occurred years earlier as a result of a series of missteps that led to allegations that American's workplace was a hostile and unwelcoming environment. Those events led to the establishment of the diversity committee and the strengthening of our workplace rules to ensure that all employees were treated with respect and dignity. At that time, American instituted a zero-tolerance policy, referred to as Rule 32, under which employees were disciplined or terminated for taking any action or using any language that was deemed to constitute "hate-related" conduct.

Given Roger Staubach's celebrity status, we frequently asked him to attend employee diversity events. Attendance skyrocketed at those gatherings he attended. Staubach would willingly speak at our events, autograph footballs, and spend time chatting with employees. At one such forum held at our training and conference center, a small group of us stood talking to Staubach. There was a football on display that we intended to raffle later in the program. Much to my surprise, he picked it up and gently tossed it underhand in my direction. I caught the ball and gave it back to him. He then made a motion indicating I should go out for a pass. I shuffled a few steps back and was greeted by a football to the chest. Fortunately, I caught the ball and threw it back to him.

By this time, a small crowd had gathered to watch the Hall of Fame quarterback throw a football. Staubach then signaled that I should go out for a deep pass. I was in a suit coat and tie, but gladly obliged. I ran straight out, careful to avoid a smattering of tables and chairs, and looked over my shoulder just in time to see the ball rifling toward me. I hoped for the best, not wanting to embarrass myself. Touchdown! It was my 15 minutes of fame as a wide receiver for Captain America.

While the finance team remained focused on the fourth tenet of the Turnaround Plan (building a strong financial foundation), other members of the executive team focused on the second tenet (giving customers what they value). Over the years, we fell far behind our competitors in terms of customer service, and there was much work to be done.

One of the most glaring problems American faced was the advancing age of its fleet of aircraft. By the end of 2010, we operated a total of 914 aircraft, 620 at the main airline and 294 at American Eagle. The average age of the mainline jets was fifteen, and American's oldest fleet type, the Boeing 767s-200s, averaged twenty-four years.

A related problem centered on the type of aircraft in American's fleet. In 2003, American operated thirteen kinds of aircraft in thirty-five distinct configurations. Different aircraft types and configurations allow airlines to match the right aircraft to the right market. But if an airline slices the marketplace into too many distinct pieces, it ends up with a complex fleet configuration, one that drives higher costs throughout the company, for things like pilot training and parts inventory. That's exactly what happened to American over the years. One of the goals of the Turnaround Plan was to simplify the fleet and drive down costs associated with fleet complexity.

Older aircraft carry a number of disadvantages. First, they are much less fuel-efficient than new-generation aircraft. This is principally due to improvements in engine design, improved aerodynamics, and the use of synthetic construction materials like carbon fiber. When you're buying nearly three billion gallons of high-priced fuel every year, fuel efficiency is paramount.

The problems associated with old aircraft go far beyond fuel efficiency. For one thing, customers don't like them. This sentiment was particularly true of American's Super 80 aircraft. One of its huge drawbacks was the lack of an in-flight entertainment system. The aircraft had no seatback video monitors so customers couldn't watch movies or other programming. Customers have come to expect these systems, and when a large percentage of our fleet had none (at that time), it was a big competitive disadvantage. On multiple occasions, we debated the cost effectiveness of retrofitting the Super 80 with an in-flight entertainment system. Each time we concluded the same thing—it was cost prohibitive.

Another problem with the Super 80 was legroom in the first-class cabin. We measure the amount of space between seats on every aircraft type in both the coach and first-class cabins and compare it to our competitors on a regular basis. The seat spacing is called "pitch," and is measured in inches. At American, pitch ranges from a low of thirty-one inches in coach to sixty-four inches in the first-class cabin of large international aircraft. On some competitor airlines, like Spirit, pitch drops to a meager twenty-eight inches. For American, the pitch in first class of the Super 80 was only thirty-nine inches.

Pitch is something that receives a lot of attention from airline execs. It is consistently the subject of heated debate, particularly between the finance and marketing departments. Pitch greatly affects passenger comfort but also has a direct bearing on profitability. The near-impossible riddle to solve is the correct mix between comfort and revenue. On one hand, less pitch equals more seats, and more seats should equate to more revenue. But as pitch decreases, passengers complain and move business to competitors. The battle is even fiercer in the first-class cabin. A generous amount of pitch is essential to attract high-paying corporate customers. But as pitch increases, the total number of seats available for sale decreases. It is a constant tug of war.

Consequently, airlines are forever modifying aircraft cabins in search of the holy grail of pitch. In February 2000, American introduced "More Room Throughout Coach," a program that increased pitch throughout the coach cabin on all aircraft. The program, dubbed MRTC, was rolled out with great fanfare, including a clever advertising promotion centered on employees throwing seats out of the aircraft and onto the tarmac. The program was a big hit with passengers. They loved the product. There was only one problem. It didn't work.

The lost revenue from fewer seats was predicated on the theory that passengers would willingly pay slightly higher fares in exchange for more pitch. But we were dead wrong. Passengers wanted the extra legroom but most didn't want to pay for it. Four years after introducing MRTC, we abandoned the project and put the seats back on the aircraft.

Just as we unraveled MRTC, United Airlines introduced "Economy Plus," a program that increased pitch in the first several rows of the coach cabin. In Chicago, where both American and United have hubs and are fierce competitors, United rolled out an advertising campaign designed to poke fun at our decision. In one print ad, there was an illustration of a man bent into a cube. The caption read "Fly American, and you could kick yourself. Literally." Initially, we thought "Economy Plus" was as stupid as MRTC. We were wrong. In March 2012, we adopted a similar program called Main Cabin Extra, and in the summer of 2017, American introduced a new product called Premium Economy with wider seats and more legroom on international flights. And so it goes in the world of airline seat pitch.

The problems with the Super 80 aircraft were only going to grow worse over time. We knew the time had come to replace them, along with other old, inefficient aircraft in our fleet. But the decision to purchase new aircraft carries an enormous capital commitment with long-term implications for the company. Given our weak financial condition, the decision was difficult but one we could not ignore.

There are two primary aircraft manufacturers in the world— Boeing and Airbus. Boeing is headquartered in Chicago, but its largest manufacturing facility is located just north of Seattle in

Everett, Washington. The Everett facility is billed as the world's largest building. Airbus is based in Toulouse, France, and has manufacturing facilities in a number of countries, including France, Germany, Spain, and the United Kingdom. It recently opened an assembly plant in Mobile, Alabama. There are other manufacturers of jet aircraft, including Embraer in Brazil and Bombardier in Canada, but they manufacture mostly smaller commuter-type aircraft. Together, Boeing and Airbus control the vast majority of the world's mainline commercial jet aircraft market.

Many airlines decide to purchase aircraft exclusively from one of these manufacturers, but not both. For instance, Southwest Airlines and Alaska Airlines operate Boeing aircraft only, while Spirit Airlines and Virgin America (now merged into Alaska Airlines) operate Airbus products only.

Historically, American didn't want to rely on a single manufacturer, so we divided our big jet purchases between Douglas Aircraft and Boeing. The first jet aircraft we bought was the Boeing 707, and Boeing's 727 later became a mainstay of our fleet. When it came time to buy a wide-body jet, we concentrated on the Douglas DC-10. After McDonnell and Douglas merged to form the McDonnell Douglas Corp., we purchased updated DC-9s, called the MD-80 or Super 80. For larger jets, we began ordering the single-aisle Boeing 757s and two-aisle 767s in the 1980s.

There were exceptions to the Boeing-Douglas jet duopoly. We operated a fleet of thirty-five wide-body Airbus A300 aircraft from 1988 through 2009. This came about when Airbus offered a deal to Bob Crandall that he couldn't pass up—an enormously attractive "lease to purchase" agreement. Crandall decided to diversify our fleet despite inherent drawbacks of operating more than one fleet type. It was a real coup for Airbus. The deal represented the largest order of Airbus aircraft at that time.

Similarly, in 1989, we ordered seventy-five Fokker F100 jets because we thought we needed a small mainline airplane with about one hundred seats. The Fokker ended up being a terrible airplane for us and we grounded the fleet beginning in 2002. That left us with an all-Boeing fleet (except for the thirty-five Airbus aircraft) after Boeing purchased McDonnell Douglas in 1997.

Negotiations involving a purchase of new aircraft are nothing akin to buying a new car. There are complicated aircraft capability considerations that must be addressed. These include aircraft type, e.g., narrow-body aircraft, midsize or wide-body; aircraft range, i.e., how many miles can it fly on a tank of jet fuel; the number of passengers it can accommodate; what markets it is going to fly; the number of aircraft required; and aircraft delivery dates. The questions are endless and all involve painstaking work and analysis.

As negotiations with the aircraft manufacturers got underway, we focused our discussions first with Airbus, not Boeing. We made this decision despite the fact that American had entered into a twenty-year "preferred supplier" agreement in 1996 that required American to purchase jet aircraft exclusively from Boeing (except commuter aircraft). Because Boeing made a commitment to the European Union (after 1996) that it would not seek to enforce exclusivity agreements, we didn't expect that Boeing would use the preferred supplier agreement as a weapon to exclude Airbus from the competition for American's business.

At the outset of the bidding war between Boeing and Airbus, American had an all-Boeing fleet. Oddsmakers would have given Boeing the advantage, but that didn't seem to concern Airbus officials. They put forward an aggressive price proposal and we used it to put pressure on Boeing to improve its offer. Despite the size of the deal and its complexity, negotiations advanced at an accelerated pace.

Our new aircraft deal was announced on July 20, 2011, and the results surprised nearly everyone. The aircraft purchase terms offered by Boeing and Airbus, including their respective offers to provide financing at favorable terms (despite our weakened financial position), were extremely attractive. As a result, we decided to accelerate our fleet replacement plan by purchasing large numbers of new aircraft from both suppliers. Combined, the transaction ended up being the single largest commercial aircraft purchase in the history of aviation.

The final deal was valued at over sixteen billion dollars. It included a firm order for two hundred Boeing 737 aircraft, with an option to purchase an additional one hundred. On the Airbus side, we agreed to a firm order for 260 A320s (with the ability to mix and match A319s and A321s) and an option for an additional 365 aircraft. Deliveries began in 2013 and continue today. The deal fully addressed American's aging aircraft problem and positioned us to have one of the youngest fleets in the airline industry for years to come. And the vast number of options gave us enormous flexibility for future growth. It was this latter point—growth opportunity—that we hoped would serve as a catalyst for new contracts with organized labor.

Employees, particularly those represented by organized labor groups, usually greet aircraft deals with unbridled enthusiasm. New aircraft typically translates to growth, and growth equals more jobs. For pilots, growth brings with it the opportunity to fly new and larger aircraft and to move from the co-pilot seat to the coveted captain's seat on the left side of the cockpit. That's when pilots hit the jackpot, with annual pay climbing to well over two hundred thousand dollars for the captain of a Boeing 777 or 787, our largest aircraft.

On the day we announced the largest aircraft deal in history, we remained mired in contract negotiations with all three of our unions. We quickly realized that the new aircraft deal was not going to alter the pace of the negotiations.

CHAPTER 9

OUT OF OPTIONS

After five years at the bargaining table, we were unable to bring a single labor agreement to the finish line. Like ships passing in the night, labor and management had vastly differing views of what a new contract looked like. On labor's side of the ledger, they demanded contracts that not only restored the concessions granted in 2003, but provided substantial wage increases for their members. On management's side, we offered pay increases, but demanded additional work rule improvements.

During the previous eight years, most of our major competitors successfully reduced their labor costs in bankruptcy to levels far below the cost savings we achieved in 2003. In fact, during the years between the 2001 terrorist attacks and the start of 2011, some two dozen airlines either ceased operations or filed for bankruptcy. The surviving carriers invariably came out of bankruptcy with lower labor costs.

By 2011, American was saddled with the highest labor costs of any major airline. We estimated our annual labor cost disadvantage (compared to our major competitors) at 800 million dollars and there was no way we could continue operating with such a significant cost disadvantage. Hence, it was imperative that we unload the "brick in our backpack" that Jeff Brundage had articulated so well (to the anger of employees who didn't like being considered bricks).

Putting aside bankruptcy, there were only two ways to unload the brick: We needed to sign new lower-cost labor agreements, or wait for our competitors' labor costs to rise over time. We prayed that one of these two alternatives would come to pass and rescue us as we inched ever closer to the cliff. While we continued to push for new contracts with labor, we hoped (and sincerely believed) that our competitors' costs would rise to meet ours. We referred to this latter approach as the "labor convergence plan."

The idea behind labor convergence is pretty simple. In a highly competitive industry like the airline business, most competitor labor costs fall within a band. No one can afford to be far outside the band, either too high or too low. If labor costs are too high, the company's financial results most often lag its competitors. If they are too low, labor demands parity and it is difficult to attract workers willing to be paid so much less than their counterparts. At any given time, one company may have substantially higher costs than its competitors as a consequence of signing a new labor agreement, or substantially lower costs as it nears the end of a contract. Allowing for these differences, over time, labor costs in the industry largely mirror one another.

By 2011, most of the labor contracts of our principal competitors were either open for negotiation or soon would be. Those carriers (with their lower labor costs) were profitable and we knew labor would pressure those airlines for substantial wage increases. All we needed was enough time for this to happen.

The problem for us was abundantly clear—labor convergence was not playing out as planned. Our board listened patiently at each meeting as Brundage described the status of carrier negotiations (as best he could glean from publicly available information). On each occasion, the board was left feeling hopeful that other airlines' costs would soon rise.

Apart from the hoped-for labor convergence, the second pillar of our effort focused on signing new labor contracts with each union. In particular, we needed a deal with our pilots. After five years of negotiations, we decided to make a final appeal directly to the pilot workforce, rather than allow union leadership to filter, and perhaps distort, our message.

On Monday, November 14, 2011, we delivered a comprehensive proposal to the APA, along with an elaborate update directed to individual pilots. American's message was a straightforward appeal to get a deal finished immediately:

> *Company and APA negotiators have spent several weeks in intensive bargaining sessions in an effort to conclude more than five years of negotiating...Our goal has been to put a tentative agreement in our pilots' hands and give them a chance to vote on it...*
>
> *APA negotiators haven't offered viable responses to numerous options that company negotiators have suggested as possible solutions. Instead of waiting and letting more precious time slip by, the Company elected to put a comprehensive proposal on the table today...*
>
> *Our proposals offer pay raises, maintain industry-leading benefits, increase job protections, prevent outsourcing, and create a framework for growth...*

Later that evening, a union official told *The Dallas Morning News* reporter Terry Maxon that he could see no way that the APA board of directors would send the proposal to members, or that members would approve it if the board decided to do so. According to Maxon, various board members said they wouldn't be rushed into a "quick, bad decision" just because American feels an urgency now to do a deal.

The next day, we gathered with the American Airlines board for our regularly scheduled meeting at the Four Seasons hotel in Irving, Texas, located just 15 minutes from American's headquarters. Midway through the meeting, as Bev Goulet walked the board through an array of complicated graphs on a PowerPoint presentation, she was interrupted by the hand-delivery of a letter addressed to Gerard Arpey from the Allied Pilots Association. That letter, dated November 15, 2011, contained the APA's response to our comprehensive offer made the day earlier. It proved to be the last straw on the camel's back.

Until that moment, the company and the board remained hopeful that a new pilot contract was close at hand, to be quickly followed by new contracts with the APFA and TWU. By a vote of 17-1, APA leadership rejected the company's proposal. The letter to Gerard read, in part, as follows:

> *APA leadership shares your desire to conclude negotiations expeditiously and we remain focused on reaching an agreement that is good for our pilots and good for the airline...*
> *Although management's most recent proposal does not sufficiently address our pilots' most critical negotiating priorities, we are nevertheless committed to reaching a mutually beneficial agreement through good faith bargaining at the earliest opportunity.*

On its face, the letter seems benign, citing APA's desire to continue negotiations and reach a new agreement. What the APA did not appreciate is the degree of the board's concern over the inability to conclude a satisfactory agreement with the APA, let alone the APFA and TWU. Given the APA's refusal to allow its members to even vote on the company's proposal, there was no clear path forward and no end in sight. It tested the board's patience to the breaking point. Now, all bets were off. The board's attitude hardened faster than cement on a hot Texas afternoon. American Airlines was headed to bankruptcy.

By the conclusion of the meeting, I had my marching orders—be prepared to file bankruptcy papers by the end of November. That gave us a narrow two-week window to be ready for filing. It was a mammoth undertaking. Like the face that launched a thousand ships, the union's letter and its unwillingness to budge launched a thousand tasks for completion in just fourteen days.

The next two weeks were filled with long days and nights as we prepared the necessary papers for a filing. Unlike the events in 2003, we kept our planning quiet. Our position would be worse if employees, trade vendors, and customers knew that bankruptcy was imminent. We were forced to include a large army of people in the preparatory work from almost every department in the company. In addition, we had what seemed like an even larger army of outside bankers, lawyers, and consultants working on the project.

On the legal side, we again looked to Weil Gotshal to lead the effort, with Harvey Miller, Steve Karotkin, and Alfredo Perez heading up the legal team. On the investment banking side, we engaged Rothschild & Co. Christopher Lawrence and Homer Parkhill led that team. The list of consultants included experts in public relations, media, government affairs, tax, aircraft ownership, and labor relations. With all these people scurrying to complete the one thousand tasks, it is a small miracle that news of our preparations remained secret.

A critical question requiring an immediate decision was the selection of venue. Our choices came down to Texas and New York. If we had filed in 2003, we decided that New York was the best locale because of the court's experience with large bankruptcy cases. This time around, I, along with Kathy Koorenny, my associate general counsel and day-to-day bankruptcy point person, decided to take a fresh look at the issue.

In one respect, Texas was clearly the favored locale. Texas is our principal place of business and a filing in Fort Worth or Dallas would give us hometown advantage. We believed that a Texas court would treat the company fairly and work diligently to ensure our successful reorganization. A Texas venue would also prove more convenient and accessible to management for court appearances. But ease of access cut both ways. With some 25,000 local employees, we envisioned employee rallies, picket lines, and protests, with the potential for a circus-like atmosphere at the courthouse and in the media.

The other logical venue was the Southern District of New York, a favored locale for many of the country's largest corporate bankruptcies. The courts of the Southern District are sophisticated and accustomed to handling complex bankruptcies. In addition, the Second Circuit Court of Appeals (where the Southern District is located) has a more complete set of judicial opinions interpreting the bankruptcy code than does the Fifth Circuit (where the Texas courts are located). Many of those judicial decisions interpret the code in a manner favorable to a debtor and it was unclear whether the Fifth Circuit would adopt the reasoning of the Second Circuit.

As Koorenny and I struggled with the venue question, we received substantial input from attorneys on both sides of the aisle. One of our most trusted advisors over the years was Dee Kelly. Kelly was a former AMR board member and the founding partner of Kelly Hart & Hallman in Fort Worth. His law firm represented American over the years in a series of high stakes litigation and corporate matters. I often joked that we never crossed the Fort Worth city limits without first consulting Kelly. We had several conversations concerning venue and his views on the subject were crystal clear. Kelly told me that Fort Worth was a "hell of a lot better place to file" and that "those New York lawyers charge too damn much." He then assured me that we would be treated well in Fort Worth. Kelly's parting words were, "I can do a much better job for half the price."

The East Coast contingent, Harvey Miller and Steve Karotkin, strongly favored the New York venue. They believed it carried less risk. In the end, Koorenny and I reluctantly concurred with the Weil attorneys' preferred venue. The filing was set for New York City.

We made no further progress with labor during the intervening two weeks. Nothing gave us hope that we could avoid a filing. On the weekend of November 25, I flew to New York to complete the journey I began in 2003. Wary that I would alert employees to the impending action, I flew on Delta to Newark (N.J.).

Monday morning, we held a special board meeting at Weil Gotshal's New York office. We needed to make sure everyone was aligned with the plan to file for bankruptcy. Bev Goulet and I remained in New York while Arpey, Horton, and others returned to Texas. That evening, we convened our board again for a brief telephone call. During that call, the AMR board of directors voted to file for Chapter 11 protection. The vote was unanimous.

CHAPTER 10

DIFFICULT DAYS

The November 29, 2011, filing—so low-key in its execution—kicked off a two-year odyssey. It was unlike anything I had experienced in my professional life. Days and nights merged into a blur of strategy discussions, conference calls, and negotiations. There wasn't a holiday, birthday, anniversary, or Super Bowl party that wasn't interrupted by a panicked phone call or email with demands for immediate resolution of the crisis de jour. It was two years filled with a mixture of emotions—hope, despair, hostility, suspicion, humor, and acrimony.

Concurrent with the vote to file bankruptcy proceedings, the AMR board of directors was forced to address a potential change in leadership at the company. Ever since Gerard Arpey assumed the role of CEO in 2003, he made clear his dislike of the bankruptcy process. Following the board meeting on November 15 that set us on the path to bankruptcy, Arpey faced a monumental decision—guide the company through bankruptcy or retire from the company he loved so much.

As the filing date grew near, Gerard and I discussed on many occasions whether he was the right person to lead the company through Chapter 11. It would be difficult for him to leave after a career devoted to one company. American Airlines was everything to Arpey.

The decision would have been easier for Gerard if he had lost the board's confidence. But he had the full support of the board and it was his decision alone. If he left, it would be of his own accord. He struggled with the idea of leaving the company. In the end, he acknowledged to me that he did not have it in his heart to do the things required in a bankruptcy proceeding.

After much soul-searching, on the evening of November 28, 2011, Arpey elected to retire from the company, effective immediately.

Not many people in the business world shared Gerard's view about the morality of using the bankruptcy laws as a business tool to walk away from contractual obligations to vendors and employees. Michael Lindsay, the president of Gordon College, who at that time was writing a book about executive leadership, interviewed Arpey and subsequently wrote an op-ed column for *The New York Times* published on November 30, the day after American filed for bankruptcy. Lindsay had this to say about Arpey's stance on bankruptcy:

> Over the last eight years, I have interviewed hundreds of senior executives for a major academic study on leadership, including six airline CEOs. Mr. Arpey stood out among the 550 people I talked with not because he believed that business had a moral dimension, but because of his firm conviction that the CEO must carefully attend to those considerations, even if doing so blunts financial success or negates organizational expediency. For him, it is an obligation that goes with the corner office.

Lindsay went on to conclude that Arpey may have been the only airline CEO who "regarded bankruptcy not simply as a financial tool, but more important, as a moral failing" and that "it is refreshing to see a CEO leave a position with honor even as he loses a long-fought battle."

Immediately upon Gerard's resignation, the board elected Tom Horton that same night as the new chairman and CEO of American Airlines. Like Don Carty and Gerard Arpey, I knew Horton well. Except for a short stint as CFO at AT&T, Tom was practically a "lifer" at the company. Gerard convinced Horton to return to American in 2006 as CFO and promoted him to president in 2010. They were good friends and both enjoy a passion for fly fishing and piloting their own personal aircraft.

Horton fit the persona of an American Airlines CEO—tall, thin, and athletic. Horton dressed impeccably, like he had just finished a catalog shoot for Brooks Brothers. Horton's neckties were perfectly knotted and his crisp white shirts had so much starch they could stand at attention. Like a Russian chess master, Horton is a strategic thinker, always three steps ahead of the pack.

Horton did not share Arpey's view about bankruptcy. He considered Chapter 11 an effective business tool and was an unabashed proponent of the decision to file. Likewise, unlike 2003, this time around I strongly favored bankruptcy and was pleased Horton and I were on the same page. Horton explained his, and the board's, rationale in a news release issued the morning we filed:

> *This was a difficult decision, but it is the necessary and right path for us to take—and take now—to become a more efficient, financially stronger, and competitive airline.*
>
> *...Our very substantial cost disadvantage compared to our larger competitors, all of which restructured their costs and debt through Chapter 11, has become increasingly untenable given the accelerating impact of global economic uncertainty and resulting revenue instability, volatile and rising fuel prices, and intensifying competitive challenges.*

Not surprisingly, there was a chorus of voices critical of the bankruptcy filing. By that time it didn't really matter. The deed was done and there was no turning back. We were now in the belly of the beast and had a job to do, one that we hoped to complete quickly and efficiently. I was the company's chief legal officer for the bankruptcy proceedings and my good friend and colleague, Bev Goulet, was named chief restructuring officer.

It was a good thing I liked Bev because we would work together nearly every day for the next two years. She is an attorney by training and joined American in 1993 as associate general counsel for corporate finance. After six years in legal, Goulet made the improbable move to the corporate development group in the treasury department, an assignment typically reserved for the company's large bullpen of MBA graduates. She performed so well that she was promoted to vice president and treasurer just three years later. Goulet has an enormous capacity to merge financial acumen with a common-sense approach to problem solving. To top it off, she is unflappable in times of great stress, even tempered, and possesses an extraordinary work ethic. I couldn't have picked a better partner to join me in the bankruptcy odyssey.

One quality that would see us through the enormous challenges that lie ahead was the trust that Bev and I had in one another. I could trust Bev, and she trusted me. We had a bond that saw us through some of the most difficult challenges we ever faced in our long careers at the company.

Our collective goal, one shared by outside counsel, was to successfully reorganize the business and exit from Chapter 11 within twelve months, an aggressive timeline. It didn't take long for our confidence in the timeline to waver, then vanish entirely.

As soon as we filed, we waited anxiously to learn the name of our judge. An experienced judge, one known to move quickly and efficiently, could ease our stay in bankruptcy. We made the decision to file in New York instead of Texas based, in part, on the vast experience of New York bankruptcy judges. In the old days, lawyers with enough sway could influence the selection of a judge. Such is not the standard in the Southern District. Today, as it was in 2011, the assignment is made according to a judicial "wheel" and there is no way to game the system. I kept my fingers crossed.

It didn't take long to find out how we fared. We drew the Honorable Sean Lane. I immediately peppered Harvey Miller and Steve Karotkin with questions:

"So, is he a good judge? Is he fair to debtors?"

Harvey looked at Steve, then replied, "Well, we really don't know much about him."

"OK, how much do we know?" I asked. "What big cases has he handled?"

"I don't think he's handled many big cases. In fact, I am sure yours will be by far his largest case."

By this time, I was getting a bit irritated. "Harvey, out with it. What's going on?"

"He's new. We just don't know anything about him."

I was clearly disappointed. We were only three hours into the foray of bankruptcy and already I had reasons for concern. I learned that Judge Lane was the newest judge appointed to the bankruptcy court. He joined the bench in September 2010, a mere fourteen months earlier. Judge Lane had served for the previous ten years as an assistant U.S. attorney and chief of the Manhattan office's tax and bankruptcy unit.

"This is just great," I murmured to myself. I really hoped, in fact I was led to believe, that we would get a judge who possessed a wealth of judicial bankruptcy experience. And here we were with a brand-new, untested judge handling the largest airline bankruptcy case in the history of civil aviation. We would have an opportunity to assess the damage firsthand at a hearing later that day.

In virtually all bankruptcy mega-cases, the debtor files a series of motions at the time of filing and seeks judicial orders designed to keep the debtor's business operating smoothly and without interruption. In our case, we filed a large number of "First Day" motions, including motions asking for authority to:

- Provide wages, health coverage and other benefits
- Honor passenger tickets and provide refunds
- Continue payments to critical vendors like fuel suppliers
- Continue using the cash management systems and bank accounts.

That morning we received word from the court's docket clerk setting the hearing for later that afternoon. We left Weil Gotshal's office, took the elevator to the lobby and went outside. We had three Lincoln Town Cars ready to shuttle us downtown to the courthouse.

It was never an efficient way to get to the courthouse as the traffic was always a nightmare.

I got in a car with Karotkin. It was an important day and Karotkin was set to play a big role in the day's proceedings. But that didn't stop him from cracking a few jokes on the way to the courthouse. His jokes consisted of a series of dry one-liners, typically a commentary on one or more personalities involved in the bankruptcy case. He also had an endless supply of lengthy jokes that invariably started out with "did you hear the one about...?" Over the next two years, I looked to Karotkin's jokes as a way to help me survive the madness.

The Town Cars parked in front of the courthouse, and we walked up the steps to the front door. All visitors must pass through security, including a metal detector. The federal court had a rule that prohibited anyone other than a licensed attorney from bringing a cell phone into the courthouse. Consequently, the nonlawyers would ask us to put extra cell phones in our briefcases, coat pockets, and anywhere else that we could stash such a device. It seemed odd that we readily agreed to be "cell phone mules" and violate a rule of the court without giving it a second thought.

As we entered Judge Lane's seventh floor courtroom, you would have thought that it was the site of a major motion picture premiere. Every seat in the courtroom was occupied and plenty more people were forced to watch the proceedings on live TV in an overflow room located on the sixth floor.

Even though it was a cool November day outside, the air inside the courtroom was warm and stuffy, perhaps owing to the hot air emitted by the large gaggle of attorneys assembled in the room. It was so warm that one of the Weil attorneys propped open a window to let in cool air, a ritual repeated for the next two years regardless of the season. Even in summer, on most days the air outside was cooler than the air inside the courtroom.

Everyone stood as Judge Lane entered the courtroom. For some reason, as soon as Lane uttered his introductory remarks, I felt a sense of relief. Something about his demeanor gave me confidence that we were going to be OK with this untested judge. After a litany of lawyers entered their appearance as counsel of record for various creditors and interested parties, Judge Lane turned to Harvey Miller for an opening statement.

"Today, Your Honor, is a day of mixed emotions," Miller started his remarks. "Sad, because of the event; but also a new dedication and spirit to meet the challenges ahead." Miller continued:

For the past several years, American has fought ferociously to avoid this day and not follow the other airlines that have used Chapter 11 to assist in their restructurings. However, a combination of persistent major competitive disadvantages and a distressed global economic condition have caused American to go from the largest and premier American flagship airline to the third largest network carrier. These conditions have compelled today's action to protect the inherent value of the enterprise and its approximately 88,000 employees and to continue to serve and provide its customers with the best possible service.

Miller then turned to Steve Karotkin and Alfredo Perez, one of Weil's bankruptcy partners from their Houston office, to present the array of First Day motions. Judge Lane listened to each motion and, one by one, granted the relief requested. I was feeling better by the minute. At the conclusion of the hearing, we had received the relief we needed. It was a good finish to our first day in court.

The next important event in our bankruptcy case involved the appointment of the Official Committee of Unsecured Creditors, informally called the UCC. The UCC is comprised of several of the largest unsecured creditors and is appointed by the United States Trustee. The trustee is an arm of the Justice Department and is charged with the responsibility to monitor and oversee bankruptcy cases.

The UCC plays a pivotal role in a large bankruptcy case. The committee meets with the debtor on a regular basis, reviews the debtor's business plan and its plan of reorganization, has standing to participate in court hearings, and has the right to hire professionals, like lawyers and financial analysts. The UCC's job is to maximize the payout for unsecured creditors. Often, the interests of the UCC do not align with the interests of the debtor.

Before we filed, I warned Horton and my fellow executives that the UCC plays a prominent role in a bankruptcy case. Despite that admonition, I underestimated just how much influence and power the UCC would wield in our case.

The meeting to appoint the members of the committee was held at a Sheraton hotel in Manhattan on December 5. We knew that the trustee was likely to appoint at least one of our three unions to the committee, even though none of them was an actual "unsecured creditor" at the time we filed. We were current on all financial obligations owed to our unions. Only our public statements concerning the need to reduce labor costs put them in the category of a "future" unsecured creditor.

Another interested party we had to contend with was the Pension Benefit Guaranty Corporation or PBGC. The PBGC was established in 1974 when Congress passed the Employee Retirement Security Act (ERISA). ERISA was designed to protect worker benefits in private pension plans and the PBGC is the governmental agency that administers ERISA.

The PBGC was concerned that we would seek a "distress termination" of our pension plans and dump seventeen billion dollars of liability in its lap. Officials at the PBGC had ample cause for concern. United Airlines unloaded ten billion dollars of pension liability on the PBGC in its Chapter 11 proceeding, and Delta also handed over its pilot pension plan to the agency. Fearing we might do the same thing, Josh Gotbaum, director of the PBGC, filed an application with the United States Trustee requesting appointment to the UCC.

The trustee decided to appoint nine members to the committee. I was unhappy about four of the appointees. To start with, the trustee appointed all three unions to the committee. One would have been bad enough, but all three was going to be rough. In addition, the PBGC got a seat (and the people who ended up advising the PBGC and attending the meetings for the next two years ended up being a pain in our side).

Thankfully, we were fine with the other five appointees. Two— Boeing and Hewlett Packard—were longtime suppliers and we were on good terms with both. The last three members were financial institutions—Wilmington Trust, Bank of New York Mellon, and Manufacturers and Traders Trust. We had no issues with any of them. My biggest concern was the three seats occupied by labor. With three voting members, labor held a disproportionate amount of influence over the committee, giving them ample opportunity to cause us plenty of heartburn.

With the committee fully constituted, the first order of business was the selection of professionals to assist them. In reality, these professionals would dictate the tone and tenor of the committee and its relationship with the company. On the financial side, the committee selected Moelis & Company as its investment banker, with Bill Derrough heading up the team. It also chose Mesirow Financial as its financial advisor, with Larry Lattig in the lead.

For legal counsel to the committee, imagine a roulette wheel in Las Vegas where all the numbers are black, with the exception of one lone red number. As the wheel spins, surely you would expect it to land on black. It was not our lucky day. The wheel stopped on red. Lead counsel to the committee was Jack Butler, a senior partner at Skadden Arps Slate Meagher & Flom. This was the first time Butler served as lead counsel to an unsecured creditors' committee, but he left his mark in a big way.

Butler was fifty-eight years old at the time and had the physique of a middle linebacker. In fact, for many years he was a high school and college football referee. Over the next two years, I came to know Jack Butler well and have a great deal of respect for his legal skills, but we frequently butted heads. There are many words that come to my mind to describe Jack Butler. Among them—brilliant advocate, smart as a whip, hardworking, passionate. There are others—junkyard dog, schoolyard bully, obstinate. The list goes on. We were in for one hell of a ride.

CHAPTER 11

A COLD RECEPTION

If we had any hope of exiting Chapter 11 in one year, we had to quickly develop a post-bankruptcy business plan. As we toiled away, interested parties provided ample doses of rhetoric critical of whatever we might propose.

A statement issued in January 2012, by Gotbaum on behalf of the PBGC, illustrates the point:

> *Some have suggested that American must duck its pension commitments and kill its pension plans in order to survive. We think that commitments to 130,000 workers and retirees shouldn't be disposable, that American should have to prove in court that this drastic step is necessary...*
>
> *American has more than 4 billion dollars in cash; some of that money should already have been paid into its pension plans. However, Congress, hoping to preserve plans, allowed American to defer payments. It would be a tragedy if American repaid Congress' generosity by turning around and killing the plans anyway.*

The rhetoric didn't stop there. There was plenty of speculation about a potential merger with another carrier. Various media reports cited interest from Delta, US Airways, TPG Capital, and even International Airlines Group, the parent of British Airways and Iberia. We did our best to tamp down the rumors while staying focused on the development of the business plan. Horton reminded employees "there may be opportunists who wish to acquire our company while we are in this situation."

At a February 2, 2012, meeting with the editorial board of *The Dallas Morning News,* Horton went on to say: "It's very important that this company demonstrate progress on a credible business plan. And I think we've got a great one. I could not be more fired up about the future of American Airlines beyond the restructuring."

One day before Horton's remarks to the editorial board and just sixty-five days after we filed, we were ready to present our business plan to the UCC, employees, and labor leaders. To get the ball rolling, we invited all members of the creditors' committee, along with their advisors, to our corporate headquarters for the February 1 unveiling. This ended up being the only meeting of the UCC ever held in Texas during the two-year bankruptcy case. We gathered in our "two-tiered" conference room on the sixth floor. It has a capacity for about fifty people, and every seat was occupied.

Once assembled, Bev Goulet welcomed everyone and dove headlong into the presentation. She had a lot of ground to cover so the presentation was long and detailed. We carefully crafted our business plan because we knew it would be closely scrutinized by a myriad of parties with conflicting interests and objectives. Our goal was to maximize our network revenue and take as many non-employee costs out of the business as possible. Only then did we determine the amount we needed employees to contribute by way of job, wage, and benefit cuts.

It didn't take long for Jack Butler to begin firing questions, and Harvey Miller quickly pushed back. He let Jack know that he found his line of inquiry irritating and uncalled for. There was a bite to Miller's tone and an equal bite to Butler's response. I didn't realize it at the time, but their exchange was a preview of things to come.

When the meeting ended, it didn't take long to learn what people thought of our business plan. It was met with unbridled criticism from all sides. Finding anyone who liked it was a difficult assignment.

The plan's overall target was a three billion-dollar annual improvement in operating results. We estimated that this level of improvement would give us an operating margin sufficient to bring American's results in line with its peers. Of the total, we hoped to get one billion dollars from annual revenue improvements and two billion dollars from cost savings. To achieve the revenue gains, the plan called for a 20 percent increase in departures by 2017, spread across five key markets—DFW, Chicago, Miami, Los Angeles, and New York, with international flying accounting for a substantial portion of that increase. We also contemplated revenue gains from fleet optimization and product improvements.

Wall Street analysts and industry pundits simply did not believe that we could achieve revenue enhancements of this magnitude. They protested that a 20 percent increase in flying was way too much additional capacity and that other airlines were not going to sit back and let us steal market share from them. Nor would our competitors, they claimed, be willing to watch us develop new markets and do nothing. The revenue number looked great on paper, but few people outside American's headquarters were buying it.

The criticism of the revenue plan was mild compared to the chorus of objections on the cost side.

The cost savings were slated to come from a variety of sources. Horton held a telephone news conference later that day, February 1, and had this to say about the cost savings: "Restructuring our debt and aircraft leases, grounding older airplanes, improving supplier contracts and other initiatives, and then of course necessary employee changes. Those changes are going to be very significant... those are going to be challenging..."

The "necessary employee changes" amounted to 1.25 billion dollars annually. The number was substantially greater than the size of the cost disadvantage we cited for so long to labor and the media. We frequently claimed to have an eight hundred million-dollar labor disadvantage compared to our major competitors. We were now seeking employee savings that were 50 percent larger.

And where were these savings going to come from? The answer was not pretty. We designed the underlying plan to be "fair and equitable" among all work groups so that everyone shared the pain of cost reductions. The stated goal was a 20 percent reduction in employee costs from each group, including management. The means of achieving the savings differed by work group. For example, with pilots, most of the savings came in the form of changes to work rules and pension plans. For others, it meant large head count reductions.

The proposed head count reductions took a lot of people by surprise. Overall, we targeted a reduction of thirteen thousand jobs. Of that total, the TWU, the union representing our ground workers, was set to lose nearly nine thousand people—a 40 percent reduction. Most of these jobs would be outsourced to third-party vendors. The flight attendants would lose 2,300 jobs and management head count would drop by 1,200. Management employees quietly accepted their fate, but the flight attendants and TWU members were furious.

In a statement to flight attendants, Laura Glading, president of the APFA, had this to say: "The company's proposal is even more extreme and despicable than we had anticipated; however, just as I expected and not surprisingly, the justification from management simply isn't there."

In a separate video for union members, after meeting with management, Glading minced no words:

> *The most disgusting takeaway from yesterday's meetings was the attitude of company executives. The fact that they walked into these meetings and, with a straight face, pushed that proposal across the table was the epitome of arrogance. Never once were we given credit for the sacrifices we've made over the past nine years—and continue to make. No one could explain why the eight hundred million-dollar cost disadvantage they claimed to have going into bankruptcy suddenly exploded to 1.25 billion dollars. And considering there is no credit [sic] 2.8 billion dollars. It is repulsive and I simply refuse to accept it.*

In addition to job cuts, the business plan contemplated a termination of all existing pension plans, for both active and retired employees. If successful, the PBGC would inherit almost seventeen billion dollars of American's pension liability. PBGC's Gotbaum wasn't buying it:

> *Before American takes such a drastic action as killing the pension plans of 130,000 employees and retirees, it needs to show there is no better alternative. Thus far, they have declined to provide even the most basic information to decide that.*

Not everything in the plan was doom and gloom. We made it clear that employees would receive wage increases in the future and would participate in a profit-sharing plan. That plan was fundamentally different from previous plans. The old plan kicked in after the first five hundred million dollars in pretax profits. The threshold was so high that it never once paid out during the previous decade. The new plan envisioned awards totaling 15 percent of all pretax income starting at dollar one, a huge benefit to employees.

But none of this seemed to matter. Employees were upset and angry. We understood their feelings but had little choice if we hoped to successfully reorganize the business. Horton summed it up this way:

> *As you know, our major competitors have used the restructuring process to overhaul their companies and become more competitive in every aspect of their business. Last week, these airlines announced their financial results, which highlighted, once again, a widening profit gap. Network carriers have benefited from investing their restructuring-driven profits in products and services that have helped drive revenue growth. And low-cost airlines continue to benefit from the cost efficiency that has made them a force in our industry.*
>
> *Now it is time for American to move forward on a decisive path. We are going to use the restructuring process to make the necessary changes to meet our challenges head-on and capitalize fully on the solid foundation we've put in place.*

Horton was determined to take full advantage of the provisions available under the bankruptcy laws to achieve needed changes to the business. The restructuring tools typically lead to unpleasant results for vendors, suppliers, shareholders, and employees. In most Chapter 11 cases, these constituencies suffer economic hardship as the debtor renegotiates leases and contracts, reduces employee benefits, and modifies work rules. Creditors are rarely paid in full and shareholder equity is almost always wiped out. This is precisely why Arpey found the process so distasteful.

One of the restructuring tools available to a company that files for Chapter 11 is found in Section 365 of the bankruptcy code. This provision allows the debtor to reject "executory contracts." An executory contract is any contract between a debtor and a third party that has ongoing mutual obligations. Debtors use this provision to walk away from burdensome contracts, leaving the aggrieved party with nothing more than an unsecured claim in the bankruptcy proceeding.

For big companies like American, the sheer volume of contracts can be overwhelming. American's in-house attorneys and members of the purchasing department worked with Bart Biggers and his colleagues at the Winstead law firm in Dallas to identify all of American's contracts. It was a difficult undertaking, made even more so because American did not have a central contract depository. After many months, the team uncovered over fifty thousand contracts that required review to determine which ones to reject.

Another part of the bankruptcy code, referred to as Section 1110, deals specifically with aircraft leases and aircraft financing instruments. Aircraft ownership is complex. Some airlines own their aircraft and use them as collateral for loans. Other airlines lease aircraft directly from the manufacturer or an airline leasing company. Still others purchase aircraft, then enter into a sale/leaseback with an aviation lessor. Over the years, large numbers of American's aircraft were subject to some kind of lease or mortgage.

During the bankruptcy, American used Section 1110 extensively to get rid of surplus aircraft, and to reduce the cost of aircraft leases and mortgages. American's legal and treasury departments, along with a cadre of aircraft financing experts at the prestigious New

York law firm of Debevoise & Plimpton, used Section 1110 to save the company hundreds of millions of dollars.

One of the most powerful and fundamental tools available to a debtor is found in Section 1113 of the bankruptcy code. This provision was, in many respects, at the epicenter of our bankruptcy case. It allows an employer, under certain circumstances, to reject collective bargaining agreements ("CBAs"). If our unions would not accept new labor contracts voluntarily, we intended to use this provision to force them to accept the drastic changes outlined in our business plan.

The history behind Section 1113 is fascinating. Before Section 1113 was enacted, companies in Chapter 11 used Section 365 to reject a CBA the same way a debtor rejected other contracts. After many years of rejecting labor contracts using this provision, opposition to its use came to a head in the case of *NLRB v. Bildisco & Bildisco*. This case, in which a building supply contractor threw out its union contract, went all the way to the Supreme Court. The high court affirmed the right of a debtor to use Section 365 to reject union contracts. Organized labor lobbied Congress intensively for additional protections and just five months after the *Bildisco* decision, Congress enacted Section 1113.

Section 1113 requires the debtor to satisfy a nine-step process before a judge will approve the rejection of a CBA. Basically, the debtor must prove that changes to the CBA are necessary in order for the debtor to successfully reorganize, and that the changes are fair and equitable to all affected parties.

We were not anxious to initiate the formal 1113 process. We would do so only as a last resort. Jeff Brundage, our senior vice president of human resources, summed up our goals on a February 1, 2012, conference call with reporters:

> *Our objective is absolutely to reach consensual deals as quickly as possible. Everything we're doing is geared towards that. But as you know, if we're not making progress, the next step that we'll need to take is to file the 1113 motion. But we don't have a specific timeline for that.*

Although we planned to do everything possible to get voluntary deals, we held little hope that all three unions would accept the changes being proposed by management. John Gross, American's associate general counsel of labor, understood the importance of the 1113 proceeding to the success of our bankruptcy case. Knowing that, John and I engaged 1113 counsel in the weeks leading up to the bankruptcy filing.

The prosecution of an 1113 case is a narrow specialty. Not many law firms have experienced labor lawyers who litigate these kinds of cases. Fortunately for us, we had just the right guy for the job—Jack Gallagher at the Paul Hastings law firm in Washington, D.C.

Gallagher is well known in bankruptcy circles as the best 1113 man in the business. He was in his 60s at the time and closing in on retirement. Worried that he might not want to take on such a large undertaking, I was thrilled when he agreed to handle our case. Gallagher quickly assembled other members of the firm to assist him. He added Neal Mollen, a bankruptcy specialist, and Scott Flicker, one of the firm's top litigators, to the team, along with a number of associates and paralegals. I knew we were in great hands, but also knew they faced a monumental task.

An 1113 hearing is equivalent to a trial in a civil court. Gallagher and his team were forced to write lengthy trial briefs, review thousands of pages of documents, interview witnesses, and prepare those witnesses for trial testimony. And here's the kicker—they had to do everything in triplicate. We intended to file 1113 motions against each of the three unions at the same time, and the evidence was unique to each union. This meant three simultaneous trials in Judge Lane's courtroom. John Gross threw every available company resource into the project and Gallagher did the same with his resources at the law firm. We all wanted to get into court immediately if negotiations for a consensual deal with the unions failed, but we needed to be fully prepared when it came time to file the motion.

As expected, we made scant progress in contract talks with our unions. In fact, the APA attempted a novel maneuver designed to delay or disrupt the 1113 process. The APA filed a lawsuit in which the union asked Judge Lane to rule that the National Mediation

Board retained jurisdiction over contract negotiations. If the lawsuit succeeded and we were forced to revert to the prolonged and complicated negotiating rules under the Railway Labor Act, any hope of a quick resolution under 1113 would be lost.

We filed a motion on March 9, 2012, to dismiss the lawsuit and the APA countered with a request for a summary judgment in its favor. On March 22, Judge Lane assembled everyone in his Manhattan courtroom to battle it out. Our lawyer, Harvey Miller, warned the judge up front that American couldn't wait any longer.

"Despite the strong desire on the part of American and the debtors for a consensual resolution, time is of the essence. Means have to be adopted to stem the monthly operating losses that may equal or exceed 100 million dollars," Miller told Judge Lane. "It is in this context that American has concluded that unless there is a profound change in the proposals of the unions, it has no other alternative but to initiate within the next week the statutory process provided by Section 1113 of the bankruptcy code."

That same morning, we sent a letter to employees echoing Harvey's warning in court and alerting them of our plans. "With cumulative losses of 10 billion dollars over the past ten years—and more than 1 billion dollars in 2011 alone—as well as our now stronger competitors continuing to benefit from their own restructurings, we face mounting financial pressures and real threats in the market," Jeff Brundage wrote in the letter. "We must act quickly to put the business plan in place. Continued delay and distractions are not only counterproductive, but come at real risk to the jobs and livelihoods of thousands of employees."

While we battled the APA lawsuit and continued efforts to negotiate new deals with our unions, we had numerous fires burning on other fronts. We all believed that terminating our employee pension plans was a key component to our reorganization efforts. However, the PBGC and Gotbaum, with support from American's union leaders, challenged our position, saying we hadn't proven the need to dump the pensions.

The standard set forth in federal pension law establishes a high bar for termination. We would have to prove that we would be unable to remain in business absent a termination of our pension plans. To help us build a case for termination, we needed attorneys steeped in pension law. Like so many areas of the law, the intricacies of ERISA and the PBGC are highly specialized fields. For this project, we turned to Gary Ford at the Groom Law Group in Washington, D.C. Ford and his firm are experts in pension law.

It didn't take long for Ford to reach a conclusion. With 4 billion dollars in cash, a robust business plan, and a history of making huge pension contributions even during the years we lost billions of dollars, there was virtually no chance we could meet the statutory burden for termination. It was an answer I did not want to hear. Even worse, it was an answer I didn't relish sharing with Horton.

I learned early in my career that a bearer of bad news should always bring reinforcements. It helps dull the blow of frustration venting from the recipient. In this case, I grabbed Bev Goulet for the initial meeting with Horton, and I got Ford on the phone, along with a host of in-house pension experts, for a follow-up discussion. Our recommendation was pretty clear—freeze, not terminate, the existing pension plans. Freezing the plans means that the company remains obligated to fulfill all pension obligations accrued through the date of the freeze, but does not continue to accrue liability going forward. In the end, Horton concurred with the recommendation. It was a monumental decision, one valued at 17 billion dollars.

On March 12, 2012, we announced our decision to freeze, not terminate our pension plans. Needless to say, labor leaders were overjoyed, employees ecstatic, and our friend Josh Gotbaum at the PBGC reveled at the news. Inside the executive ranks, we were not so pleased. A mere five weeks after unveiling our business plan, we found ourselves dumping one of its fundamental elements. It was not an auspicious beginning.

The "less-than auspicious" beginning of our Chapter 11 case concerned Horton. He looked to me for leadership on legal strategy and to Goulet for leadership as chief restructuring officer. I would often call Tom at home to discuss the latest twists and turns, and to seek his approval on a raft of important decisions that cropped up on a daily basis. After one such discussion in the early days of the case, he suggested we meet to take stock of our progress. We met one Sunday afternoon at the Dallas Country Club.

I arrived at the country club around 4 p.m. on the day of our planned meeting. The temperature that afternoon was cool, yet pleasant. We sat outside, ordered a beer, and got down to business.

Horton outlined his frustrations with the direction of the case and the perceived lack of progress. He laid out his concerns about what he deemed inconsistent advice from outside counsel. He asked whether I was pleased with the composition of our legal team and if I thought we were getting the best advice available in the marketplace. Tom also cited the lack of coordination among the vast sea of consultants and advisors working on our case. It didn't take a rocket scientist to figure out that he wasn't too pleased.

I was in a delicate position. I agreed with many of the issues Horton raised and did my best to assuage his concerns. I reminded Tom that several of the recent developments in the case were outside the control of our legal advisors. For instance, it wasn't Weil's fault that the U.S. Trustee decided to name all three unions to the UCC, and it wasn't Groom's fault that we couldn't meet the legal test for termination of our pension plans.

Horton listened, but I could tell he wasn't buying what I was selling. I reiterated what he already knew—it was my responsibility to advance our Chapter 11 case in the most efficient and expeditious manner possible. I planned to do exactly that.

As we gazed out at the manicured expanse of the country club, both of us would have gladly swapped our cold beers for a crystal ball. Neither of us had any idea what lay before us. Things were about to heat up in a big way and the source of our discontent was located one thousand miles directly west of Dallas-Fort Worth.

CHAPTER 12

PHOENIX IS CALLING

Friday, April 20, 2012, started out like every other day since we had entered Chapter 11 almost five months earlier—nonstop strategy sessions and meetings, lengthy phone calls with outside counsel, a mountain of trial briefs and documents to review, coupled with the knowledge that a crisis du jour would surface before the day was done. Little did we know that it would emanate from our competitor in Phoenix.

Shortly after we filed, chatter and speculation abounded concerning the prospect of American combining with another carrier. On January 13, 2012, *The Wall Street Journal* reported that Delta, then the world's largest carrier, US Airways Group, and TPG Capital, a private equity firm, were each assessing potential bids for American. According to *The Journal*, people inside Delta had conducted preliminary antitrust analysis and concluded that a deal (with some concessions) might be possible.

One day earlier, Doug Parker, US Airways' CEO, called Horton and told him that his company had hired financial advisors and lawyers to help evaluate potential merger alternatives. Whatever Horton might have been thinking privately, early on, he scoffed publicly at the idea. At an editorial board meeting with *The Dallas*

Morning News on February 2, Horton had this to say about a possible combination with US Airways:

> *Let's go back and look at history a bit. This is not US Airways' first attempt at this. This is a small company, very strategically limited, I would argue—not any international flying, hubs of less strategic importance.*
>
> *This will be their fourth try at this: Twice for United, once for Delta while they were restructuring, now American. I'm not sure what's in the water out there in Phoenix. Maybe it's the cactus. I don't know what it is.*

To be clear, we were not opposed to a potential merger partner. For us, it was a question of timing. Horton was a huge proponent of consolidation in the industry and had long touted the benefits of a merger under the right circumstances. In fact, three months before we filed, Horton met with Parker at an industry event and told him that a potential deal between our two carriers might make sense after American secured new labor agreements. But the timing had to be right, and a merger during a bankruptcy proceeding wasn't the right time—at least not to our way of thinking.

Beginning in February, and continuing through April, we picked up information suggesting that US Airways executives were talking directly to our union leaders, with a few published reports claiming that Doug Parker and president Scott Kirby were trying to piece together preliminary term sheets with them. At the time, we didn't take these reports seriously because it seemed inconceivable that labor would fall in bed with US Airways.

With Parker's call to Horton, the media speculation, and the hint that our unions might be speaking with US Airways, I was concerned. I'm not a suspicious person by nature, but I wondered whether there was more at play than appeared at first blush. Our legal advisors said to ignore it, said it was a distraction and that nothing would come of it. But something about it felt a lot like poison ivy—the more you scratch it, the more it itches.

On April 17, the "M" word was a hot topic at a dinner hosted by the advisors to the UCC at Skadden's New York office. Tom Horton,

Bev Goulet, and I attended the meeting, along with the Weil Gotshal and Rothschild advisors. For the UCC, Jack Butler and Jay Goffman from Skadden were there, along with representatives from Moelis and Mesirow.

One of the attendees from Weil Gotshal was Tom Roberts. Roberts is a renowned corporate M&A (mergers and acquisitions) lawyer and he became a central figure in the case as soon as merger speculation heated up. Horton and Roberts knew each other well, dating to work they did together on the TWA acquisition in 2001. I didn't have previous dealings with Roberts and knew little about him. I was skeptical of his involvement because I was concerned that his close relationship with Horton might create difficulties for me as general counsel. I didn't need Horton running directly to Roberts as issues arose, and I sure didn't need Roberts whispering in Horton's ear, leaving me to play catch-up. I decided to watch and wait.

The agenda for the meeting was straightforward, as were the battle lines. The UCC wanted us to consider merger alternatives now, and we wanted to wait until we were safely out of bankruptcy before considering a possible combination. Horton viewed a merger inside bankruptcy as terribly disruptive to the Chapter 11 process, one that would force American to negotiate from a position of weakness. Waiting until the bankruptcy was complete, with our financial house in order, would allow us to negotiate from a position of strength.

Butler pushed back, arguing that the debtor's estate, and by definition its creditors, would benefit tremendously from the enhanced value created by a transaction inside bankruptcy (despite the fact that a merger after American emerged from bankruptcy would have created similar incremental value). He said the UCC wanted a written "protocol agreement" setting forth how and when merger discussions would proceed.

Butler didn't stop there. He demanded that we meet with US Airways face-to-face. We made it clear that such a meeting was out of the question. When asked whether any of the UCC advisors had yet met with US Airways, we were told no, there had been no such meetings.

Unbeknownst to us, they had been talking with US Airways behind our backs. Various members of the UCC advisors had already met twice with US Airways—on March 9 and April 9. It was a stacked deck and we didn't even know it. The dinner adjourned with no resolution.

The next day, Goulet and I met with the Weil attorneys (again at Skadden's office) to figure out our next move. I soon realized that our advisors were not on the same page.

Harvey Miller repeated the same advice he gave the first time that media reports surfaced about US Airways: "Ignore them. Do not engage." Regarding the UCC's request for a protocol agreement, he gave the same cautionary advice: "Do not let the UCC dictate how we proceed with our case, or they will take control of the process."

Tom Roberts had a different mind-set. He argued that merger discussions would take place with or without us so we needed to set the ground rules and lead the process. The two of them continued sparring, both passionately dedicated to their respective views. Tensions flared and harsh words followed as Harvey yelled at Roberts, "You are fucking up this case" and stormed out of the room. I recall looking over at Bev Goulet as if to say, "What was that all about?" No one said anything until Steve Karotkin broke the ice in typical Karotkin fashion, "Well, what's for lunch?"

By that time, every waking moment was consumed by one question—what do we do about US Airways? The issue was debated endlessly. Initially, Horton and the executive team advocated a swift and bold effort to discredit the merger buzz, just as Delta did years earlier when it fended off a US Airways bid with its successful "My Delta" campaign. The outside legal and financial advisors thought otherwise. They cautioned against alienating the UCC and galvanizing labor's position. If our business plan is superior, they argued, then it would triumph in the end. Besides, no one believed that Parker and Kirby could actually reach any kind of accommodation that would pacify our three labor groups, each of which had a long list of demands.

We waited for the other shoe to drop. It dropped in a big way on April 20. On that day, Doug Parker placed a telephone call to Tom

Horton, followed by an email. Our "friends" in Phoenix wanted to buy American Airlines.

The fact that Parker's company wanted to buy American Airlines made for an interesting twist of fate. Doug Parker combines an affable demeanor and a disarming smile with intelligence and a hefty measure of common sense. He is hard not to like. Parker actually got his start in the airline industry at American Airlines. He joined American's finance department in 1986 and worked alongside Tom Horton. After five years, Parker moved to Northwest Airlines before taking the CFO job at America West in 1995. Just ten days before the 9/11 terrorist strikes, Parker was named chairman and CEO of that company. America West merged with US Airways in 2005 and Parker retained the chairman and CEO posts of the newly combined airline.

In a well-documented case, Parker made an unsuccessful attempt to merge with Delta in 2006 while Delta was still in bankruptcy. Later, he also tried to merge with United Airlines, but ran into numerous obstacles and the deal never materialized.

The email from Parker was an "indication of interest" to purchase American Airlines and its parent, AMR Corporation. The nonbinding offer contemplated that AMR creditors would receive 49.9 percent of stock in the newly combined company, with US Airways shareholders controlling 50.1 percent. In addition, AMR creditors would receive an unsecured note for 1.5 billion dollars. The offer stated that the new company would retain the name American Airlines and that company headquarters would remain in Fort Worth.

There was one item in the email that came as a big surprise. Parker claimed that US Airways had signed "conditional labor agreements" or "CLAs" with all three of American's labor unions—the APA, TWU, and APFA. We didn't have to wait long to find out if Parker's claim was accurate. That same day our unions announced that they had in fact signed CLAs with US Airways.

We were dumbfounded that our labor unions would team up with US Airways. We convinced ourselves that a CLA is just what the words imply—conditional. We believed it was merely a ploy, a bit of grandstanding by labor leaders and not anything that rank-and-file employees were remotely interested in. But US Airways knew they could easily entice labor with wage increases by using a portion of future merger benefits to fund incremental labor costs, and that's precisely what they did in the CLAs.

Deciding how to respond to Parker's email was easy. We had no obligation to make the email public and had no intention of doing so. We gave our board a quick update and told them we would discuss the offer further at our regularly scheduled meeting in May.

Deciding how to respond to the announcement from labor was much more difficult. We considered lots of options, including the idea of sending a letter to all employees roundly criticizing the conditional labor deals and detailing all the reasons a US Airways merger was a bad idea. However, we recognized the danger in this approach because it would have been difficult to "walk back" such a letter if later we realized that the merger was in the best interest of our stakeholders.

In the midst of this pandemonium, my assistant, Heather Donnelly, stuck her head in my office:

"Excuse me, Gary, I need to let you know that there's a fire drill scheduled at headquarters today."

I wasn't sure I heard her correctly. "I don't understand. What are you saying?" I asked.

"Campus Security has scheduled a fire drill for later today."

I came near to exploding at Heather. "A fire drill? You've got to be kidding. Unbelievable. Here's what you do. You tell them it's canceled and it remains canceled until further notice."

I apologized to Heather later that day. We had a good laugh about it. It certainly added to the surreal nature of the day. As to the CLAs, we decided against the employee letter, but still lacked a cohesive strategy for the dealing with the tumult created by US Airways and our unions.

The original strategy of simply ignoring US Airways was not working out as hoped. It was pretty clear that Parker had no intention of walking away, and now union leadership was fully engaged. On top of that, the UCC was pushing us to explore merger opportunities.

One question that nagged at me and the Weil lawyers was whether we could take affirmative legal action to change the dynamics of the situation. We talked about different strategies and landed on one that might just work to fend off US Airways.

A debtor is entitled to an array of protections during its stay in Chapter 11. One of the fundamental protections is something called the "Automatic Stay." This provision of the bankruptcy code is like the force field of the Starship Enterprise. Among other things, the Automatic Stay prohibits parties from taking any act "to exercise control over property of the estate..." Another section of the Code (section 541) broadly defines "property of the estate" to include "all legal or equitable interests of the debtor in property."

Armed with these two provisions, we were prepared to file a motion in bankruptcy court seeking an order that prohibited US Airways and its representatives from speaking to or negotiating with our labor unions while we remained in Chapter 11. They were messing with our case and they needed to stop.

Admittedly, it was a novel theory. To succeed, we would have to convince Judge Lane that US Airways' actions were detrimental to the estate and interfered with our property rights under the bankruptcy code. Bankruptcy judges often afford great latitude to the debtor and do their best to protect the debtor's estate against intrusion by third parties. Prevailing on the motion would be an uphill struggle, but one we believed had a reasonable chance of success.

Filing the motion would send a strong message to US Airways and our unions that we would not tolerate conduct that interfered with our efforts to reorganize the business. We also hoped it might spur our unions to sign new contracts and avoid the 1113 trials set to begin on April 23, 2012. We recognized, however, that there was significant risk associated with such a filing.

First, there was a real possibility the maneuver might enrage or anger union employees and push them further into Parker's embrace. We had no idea whether the desire to merge with Parker's company was an aspiration of union leaders only or if the rank and file shared this sentiment.

The second problem was the UCC. We were certain that any effort we made to block US Airways' access to our unions would be met with great resistance by the UCC. So even if we prevailed in court, it might be nothing more than a Pyrrhic victory.

At the time, I relished the idea of filing the motion. I desperately wanted to shake things up, rather than sit back and do nothing. But when you are general counsel, there is a time to be bold and a time to be cautious. Knowing the difference is often nothing more than listening to your gut. My gut told me to hold fire for the time being and see how things played out. While we could always file the motion down the road if need be, I was pretty sure that once this ship sailed, we would never revisit the opportunity.

Meanwhile, the UCC advisors continued to push for a merger protocol agreement. Despite Harvey Miller's admonition to the contrary, I believed we would lose control of our Chapter 11 case if we did not agree to a formal process for consideration of merger scenarios. The entire weekend of April 28–29 was devoted to a series of conference calls to hammer out the terms of the agreement. Negotiations continued during the course of the following week. Miller never wavered in his belief that a protocol agreement was a terrible idea. He believed it ceded too much control to the UCC, and indirectly to Jack Butler (whom he often referred to as "His Eminence").

As issues arose, Butler got in the habit of calling me directly. I didn't mind, but Miller was really upset that Butler would dare speak to his client outside the presence of a Weil attorney. There is a legal rule that prohibits opposing counsel from speaking with the other party's client unless the client's attorney is present. The difference here is that while American Airlines was the client, I was a lawyer and did not need the usual protections offered to a layperson. I often found it productive to deal directly with Butler but it irritated Harvey Miller immensely. After one such communication, Miller called Butler and prohibited him from speaking to me without counsel present. When I found out what he had done, it was my turn to be irritated with Miller. I told him I could handle myself just fine and would not abide his request.

Finally, on May 1, 2012, we signed the Joint Exploration and Protocol Agreement. The agreement laid out a process for considering consolidation opportunities. It ran through December 28, 2012, and expressly recognized the importance of the company's independent plan. Our independent plan would serve as a base case against which alternatives could be evaluated.

One of the important provisions of the Protocol Agreement, and a source of heated debate, concerned the filing of a "plan of reorganization." The bankruptcy code confers on the debtor the exclusive right to file a plan of reorganization during the first four months after a Chapter 11 filing. The exclusivity period can be extended with court approval for a maximum of eighteen months. This exclusivity right is extremely valuable to a debtor because it gives the debtor time to reorganize its business without concern that a third party will file its own plan and disrupt the debtor's efforts. We filed for Chapter 11 on November 29, 2011, so our maximum "exclusivity" period ran through the end of May 2013.

The protocol agreement stated that we would not file a plan of reorganization before December 1, 2012, unless it had support of the UCC. The UCC was concerned that we might rush to the courthouse with an independent plan before fully examining merger alternatives. Our agreement not to file a plan before December 1 was a big concession but, unlike other demands made by the UCC advisors, I understood the basis of their concern.

Concurrent with the negotiation of the Protocol Agreement, the 1113 hearing finally got underway in Judge Lane's courtroom. It started on April 23 and continued for several weeks. We set up a "war room" at the Hilton Hotel overlooking the construction site of the new "Freedom Tower" on the grounds where the World Trade Center once stood.

On the day the 1113 hearing began, the atmosphere surrounding the courthouse was tense. Across the street in Battery Park, hundreds of employees and union supporters picketed and protested the proceedings. Given the acrimonious relationship between employees and management, our corporate security team insisted that they escort us each day from the hotel to the courtroom. I've never been escorted anywhere in my life and I didn't like it. It was unnecessary and embarrassing but out of my hands.

A successful 1113 hearing was essential to our reorganization. We desperately needed to prevail. We hoped that Judge Lane would rule in our favor and allow us to reject the collective bargaining agreements with the APFA, TWU and APA. A failed motion would set us on our heels. We filed close to two thousand pages of legal papers in support of our case.

Jack Gallagher made the opening statement on behalf of the company: "In American's view, Your Honor, this hearing is the single most important step to date in this bankruptcy case. Indeed, in our view, the outcome of this hearing will determine the course of this entire reorganization."

To prevail under Section 1113, we needed to prove that the changes we sought were "necessary" for us to successfully reorganize our business. We also were required to show that the changes were fair and equitable among all employee groups. To make our case, we called a series of witnesses to testify to the financial condition of the company, how we arrived at the 1.2 billion dollars of proposed employee changes, and how we developed the methodology behind the allocation of givebacks. Most of our witnesses were AA employees and performed well on the stand. A few did not. Despite the lackluster testimony by certain of our witnesses, I was pleased with the strength of the evidence in support of our case.

On the other side of the aisle, labor's defense of the 1113 motion was strange. It centered on the potential merger with US Airways. They argued that a merger would preclude the need for cost savings from employees. We countered that a merger was totally speculative and therefore irrelevant and of no probative value to the question before the court.

By early May, with the 1113 trial well underway, there was a major shake-up in the executive ranks of the company. Jeff Brundage, the architect of our labor strategy, announced that he would soon retire from the company. His departure was part of a broader reorganization of the executive team that included departures of Monte Ford, chief technology officer; Tom Del Valle, senior vice president of airport services and cargo; and Bob Reding, executive vice president of operations. Brundage agreed to stay on until the conclusion of the 1113 trial. The Brundage departure, in the middle of the 1113 case, was a long time in the making and not a significant disruption. In fact, Brundage remained a close advisor and a big help throughout the 1113 proceeding.

Horton named Denise Lynn to succeed Brundage. Lynn was then serving as vice president of employee relations, the department charged with overseeing labor relations under Brundage. Brundage and Lynn were polar opposites in many ways. Brundage reminds me of one of those spinning tops I used to play with when I was a kid. You pull the string and the top spins wildly until gravity brings it to a stop. The difference with Brundage is that he remains in perpetual motion, with a dizzying array of ideas and decision trees. Brundage never met an argument he couldn't twist to his advantage. I love that quality about him. On the other end of the spectrum, Denise Lynn has just as much energy as Brundage, is every bit as smart, but does so with perfect control and demeanor. She is like Mary Poppins—practically perfect in every way, complete with a pleasing British accent.

After the hearing concluded and before Judge Lane's ruling, Brundage and Lynn worked tirelessly to conclude new CBAs with each union. If successful, we wouldn't need the 1113 rejection as to any union that signed a new CBA. This would be music to Judge Lane's ears. Like any judge faced with a difficult decision, Lane was loath to rule on the 1113 motion if he could avoid doing so.

The unions were in a tight spot. They faced a classic Hobson's choice. One choice required labor to acquiesce and sign new CBAs they found unpalatable. The other choice was equally unattractive. If they did not sign new CBAs and Judge Lane ruled in our favor, the company would be free to unilaterally implement new labor terms, a consequence dreaded by union leaders.

Before the 1113 hearing commenced in April, five of the seven TWU bargaining units reached a tentative agreement with the company. By July, the two remaining TWU employee groups, the mechanics and stores employees, also concluded tentative agreements. The vote by the membership was close, with only 50.25 percent voting in favor. But a win is a win, and we were pleased.

Then, we got more good news from the flight attendants. APFA union leaders agreed to send our "last, best, and final" offer out for a vote. On August 19, we learned the results—more than 59 percent voted to accept the terms of the new contract. Three weeks later, Judge Lane formally approved the new TWU and flight attendant contracts.

The pilots were the lone holdouts. By mid-June, we were getting nowhere fast. Judge Lane suggested we give mediation a try. He enlisted one of his colleagues on the bankruptcy bench, Judge James Peck, and Peck agreed to mediate our negotiations. We met on several occasions with Judge Peck, but even he could not break the logjam. By the third week of June, we submitted another offer to the leadership, and once again they voted it down. Then, after we sweetened the deal even further, the APA relented. On June 27, the APA board, by a vote of 9-7, agreed to put our final offer out for ratification by its membership.

This development gave us renewed hope that we could get a ratified deal with our pilots without Judge Lane having to throw out their contract.

CHAPTER 13

HAVOC ON THE RUNWAY

Our optimism over the pilot deal was short-lived. When the votes were counted on August 8, 2012, 61 percent of the pilots voted against the deal. We blamed the APA board for the failed vote and they blamed us. Union leaders pointed to a series of management missteps, including a video extolling the virtues of the deal. Under APA logic, if management says the deal is good for pilots, then surely it must be bad. So maybe we should have said the deal was bad for pilots and it would have passed. Either way, it made no sense. APA leadership also attributed the failed vote to statements allegedly made by management that we wanted to merge with JetBlue, not US Airways.

The UCC and its advisors were in an uproar about the failed APA vote and demanded that Horton appear at a UCC meeting on August 14. They planned to grill him about the vote and about rumors that we were in merger discussions with JetBlue. Reuters went so far as to report that Horton had been "summoned" by the UCC to New York.

It seemed to us that the UCC advisors at times acted like petulant children, and this was one of those times. Horton threatened to boycott the meeting given the "inquisition"-type atmosphere surrounding his attendance. I thought his anger was justified, but

I pleaded with him to appear despite the air of mistrust and suspicion. The next morning, I was relieved when Horton walked into the conference room at Skadden's New York office.

When the meeting convened, Horton calmly addressed the committee's concerns about the APA vote. He also told them emphatically that we were not engaged in merger discussions with JetBlue. Afterwards, it was clear that the level of mistrust ran deep— most of the committee members, along with their advisors, did not believe a word we told them. They were convinced that we were secretly planning to merge with JetBlue. And, there was nothing we could do to convince them otherwise.

The remainder of the UCC meeting was similar to every other UCC meeting we attended during the bankruptcy. The meetings were held in a large conference room at the Skadden Arps law office in Midtown Manhattan. Each of the nine official members of the committee brought two, three, and sometimes four people to the meeting. Some were lawyers, others were financial advisors, and others just seemed to enjoy being included as part of the process. All told, there were easily forty to fifty people in attendance.

The first half of the day was typically devoted to private discussions among the committee and its advisors. Following lunch, American representatives, along with our outside lawyers and bankers, would make a series of presentations to the committee. As chief restructuring officer, Bev Goulet assumed primary responsibility to address, with equal doses of patience and diplomacy, the agenda items and issues raised by the committee.

The day following the UCC meeting was an important day. Judge Lane was set to announce his decision in the 1113 case against the pilots. I was confident of the outcome and desperately wanted this part of the bankruptcy case behind us. We arrived to a packed courthouse. I heard the words "all rise" and I knew the moment was upon us. As Judge Lane began reading his opinion into the record, I was pleased. I heard all the right words:

...The Court concludes that American has established that significant changes are necessary to the APA's collective

bargaining agreement for reorganization. Crucial to this conclusion is the undisputed fact that American labor costs for pilots are among the highest of its network competitors and that American has lost more than 10 billion dollars since 2001, including more than 1 billion dollars in 2011. The Court rejects the APA's contention that American must engage in a merger transaction before being granted relief under Section 1113 as such a notion is inconsistent with the expedited relief contemplated by the statute and the simple fact that no merger transaction has been presented to this Court. The Court also rejects the APA's related contention that American's business plan is fatally flawed and thus an improper basis for seeking Section 1113 relief. The Court finds instead that American's business plan is very similar to the business plans presented in other airline bankruptcies and thus provides an appropriate basis for establishing that significant changes are necessary to the APA's existing collective bargaining agreement.

Then, to my disappointment, the words headed south and I knew we were in trouble:

The Court concludes that American's proposed changes to furlough and codesharing have not been justified by either reference to the Business Plan or the practices of American's competitors. Given the significance of these two provisions collectively to American's proposal, the Court finds that American has not shown that the proposal is necessary as required by Section 1113. For the reasons set forth above, therefore, American's Motion to reject the collective bargaining agreements of the APA is denied.

I now had to deliver the news to Horton, and subsequently our board, that our motion to reject the pilot CBA had failed. Explaining that we prevailed on everything except two small points did nothing to lessen the blow of disappointment. Even the UCC advisors were dejected and everyone seemed to have an opinion on the matter. Some were helpful, others just annoying. Jim Millstein, an advisor to US Airways, sent out a long and strange email analogizing the situation to a Greek tragedy, complete with names and events drawn from mythology. Harvey Miller, as he was prone to do, sent a short, yet humorous, email that said it all: "Gird your loins. It will be a long battle."

Instead of languishing in despair, we quickly made the two changes that Lane found objectionable and refiled the motion two days later on August 17. At long last, at a September 4 hearing, Judge Lane granted our motion to reject the pilot contract.

With the contract rejected, we were free to implement an array of pilot work rule changes. Jack Butler and the UCC advisors pleaded with us to hold off implementing anything other than those changes universally applicable to all work groups. It was not the first time that Butler and company tried to tell us how to run the business and it would not be the last. In our view, because the pilots voted against the tentative agreement, we had no choice. To do nothing would send a message that there are no consequences for voting down the latest agreement. It would be a slap in the face to the TWU and the APFA. It was time to move forward.

We soon began implementing changes to pilot work rules. As often happens when we dare stand up to the pilots, they take out their frustrations on the airline and its customers. Without warning, flight delays and cancellations soared beginning in early September. Pilots suddenly began to report a much higher number of "maintenance" problems and "safety"-related issues. Many of these so-called issues came to light immediately before departure, maximizing the inconvenience to passengers. They also resorted to an often-used tactic of taxiing the aircraft to and from the runways as slowly as possible.

Flight delays and cancellations wreaked havoc on our flight schedule and stranded tens of thousands of passengers. The union denied that a job action was underway, but the evidence was incontrovertible. After the APA publicly defended the sudden spike in maintenance write-ups, we issued the following statement on September 28, 2012, that read in part:

The APA's press release is an outrageous and disappointing attempt to divert attention from the real issues of the operational disruption caused by some pilots' illegal job action. The kinds of issues cited in their press release are not uncommon in the industry and they are not the issue. No one at American is questioning normal maintenance write-ups.

However, certain pilots are engaging in an unlawful, concerted effort to damage the company. For the past several weeks, we have seen an unprecedented increase in pilot maintenance write ups, many at the time of scheduled departure, which are certainly not safety related. And, the number of reports where a mechanic has responded to a pilot's complaint and found nothing wrong have risen 97 percent. The unlawful conduct by some pilots includes unnecessary checks, increased and late-filed maintenance write-ups, increased block times due to slow taxiing, and circuitous routings.

We'd had enough. The pilot slowdown was costing us millions of dollars and inflicting untold pain on our customers. It was time to take legal action to enjoin the pilot slowdown. We prepared the necessary papers and got ready to file a lawsuit in Judge Lane's court. We'd seen this kind of job action before and it was always terribly disruptive.

Shortly before the 1990 holidays, a number of pilots unhappy about the slow pace of contract talks decided to foul up our operation by taxiing slowly, raising maintenance issues, and otherwise causing delays and cancellations. The effect was so bad that CEO Bob Crandall temporarily reduced American's schedule by 5 percent until the contract dispute was resolved.

A much larger and more significant disruption occurred shortly after we purchased a small carrier, Reno Air, in December 1998. The pilots were displeased that we intended to operate Reno as a separate carrier for a period of time before combining it with American Airlines. The union argued that under the APA contract, Reno pilots must be integrated immediately. While we negotiated the issue, there was a sudden spike in pilot sick calls, with other pilots refusing to voluntarily fly additional trips as they normally did. Between February 6 and 9, we were forced to cancel more than 1,600 flights due to an insufficient number of pilots to fly the aircraft.

On February 10, 1999, we sought an injunction in Dallas federal court to halt the illegal job action. U.S. District Judge Joe Kendall heard evidence from both sides. At the conclusion of the hearing, he issued a temporary restraining order against the pilots. In a decision issued in September 2000, the Fifth Circuit Court of Appeals summed up Kendall's order:

> The TRO required the defendants and anyone working for or with them to take "all reasonable steps within their power" to prevent continuation or encouragement of the sickout. The TRO also contained specific requirements: that the defendants "instruct all pilots to resume their normal working schedule," that the defendants notify all APA-represented pilots by the "most expeditious means possible" of the contents and meaning of the TRO, that the latter communication contain a directive "to cease and desist" the sick-out, that the communication be posted on the APA's web site, that the contents of the TRO ordering paragraphs be included on all telephone hotlines held by the APA, that the defendants report by noon on February 12, 1999, the methods used to effect the notice required by the TRO, and that copies of the notice and reports be furnished to American.

One would think that a court order would result in a rapid cessation of the unlawful job action. Instead, APA members elected to double down. The next day, February 11, we were forced to cancel more than 1,200 flights. The company immediately returned to Judge Kendall's court pleading that he hold the union and its officials in contempt. A hearing was held the following day and an angry Joe Kendall did exactly that—he held the union and its officials in contempt of court. He warned the union that if the job action continued, "all the assets of the union, including their strike war chest, will be capable of being safely stored in the overhead bin of a Piper Cub."

He told the union to hand over ten million dollars as damages for violating the TRO, and he assessed fines of ten thousand dollars on APA president Rich LaVoy and 5,000 dollars on vice president Brian Mayhew. In a subsequent hearing, he raised the total APA damages to 45.5 million dollars, and directed that the money be paid to American Airlines. The Fifth Circuit in its 2000 decision upheld Kendall's ruling.

Judge Kendall's February 12 order effectively ended the sick-out. In total, we had to cancel approximately 6,600 flights. The job action cost us almost 225 million dollars, nearly double the amount we paid to acquire Reno Air.

That was 1999, and here we were in 2012 faced with almost identical conduct by pilots. The decision to file for injunctive relief is not easy, but one thing was clear—we couldn't wait much longer. Our flight operation was in shambles.

The period of time between the signing of the Protocol Agreement and the beginning of the pilot slowdown—basically the entire summer of 2012—was highlighted by an almost daily skirmish with the UCC advisors concerning how and when to begin discussions with potential merger partners. Under the Protocol Agreement, we committed to examining merger alternatives, but it was silent regarding how that examination would be conducted.

We had our hands full dealing with the UCC advisors on this issue, but it proved equally difficult to wrangle a consensus among our own advisors and company executives. Throughout the months of May and June, we engaged in dozens of excruciating and mind-numbing conversations about the best path forward, complete with a remarkable number of profanity-laced outbursts. Use of the "F-bomb" became an accepted manner of speech. Whenever my level of frustration reached a zenith, I turned for advice to Rich Rothman, the same attorney at Weil that I looked to during the 2003 governance crisis and so many times in the years that followed. Rothman always provided sound guidance and, when necessary, an offer to enter the fray in an effort to resolve a difficult issue.

Often, after a long day, my cell phone would ring late at night. I typically knew who it was without looking. The caller would be Tom

Roberts. He called repeatedly to assure me that we would find a way through the morass. I could never tell whether he was reassuring me or if I were reassuring him. Either way, I abandoned my earlier reticence concerning his involvement in the case. He was a loyal and trusted advisor to me throughout.

Never had I experienced such difficulty reaching agreement among people who shared the same goal—to do what is best for the company and its constituents. But the difficulty was easy to understand. The future of the company was at stake.

Early on in the debate, Bev Goulet and I pushed for a rapid, head-on engagement with US Airways and other merger candidates. We did so knowing that such an approach carried significant risks. We worried that we might find ourselves in genuine peril if the UCC concluded that we were dragging our feet and unwilling to engage in substantive merger analysis and discussion.

It was now early July 2012 and we were worn out. We had debated, pondered, considered, reconsidered, questioned, and deliberated every conceivable idea and possibility many times over. But at long last we adopted a strategy. It was actually pretty simple. We agreed to send a letter to all employees letting them know that discussions would soon commence with US Airways and other airlines regarding a possible combination. At the same time, we would continue work on our independent plan. The independent plan would serve as a benchmark against which a merger would be evaluated. In addition, Horton planned to reach out directly to Parker and set a time to meet face-to-face.

Not everyone was pleased with the strategy, but there was no turning back. I felt a sense of relief, combined with a dose of caution. Harvey Miller sent me another of his poignant emails and his words lightened my day: "Doom is upon us. Web grows complicated. Proceed with caution."

CHAPTER 14

THE TEMPERATURE RISES

Tom Horton and Doug Parker met at the Jefferson Hotel at 6:15 a.m. on July19, 2012. The hotel is located in Washington, D.C., less than a mile from the White House. The media would later dub their breakfast meeting the "Oatmeal Summit."

While Horton and Parker didn't come to any kind of understanding during breakfast, it marked a turning point in the legitimacy of the efforts by US Airways (or in Harvey Miller's lexicon the "Phoenix Bird") to get its foot in the door. It also recalibrated the agenda and heightened the discourse, among four largely adversarial parties—American Airlines, US Airways, the unsecured creditors' committee, and American's labor unions.

When we filed for bankruptcy in the early morning hours of November 29, 2011, I certainly didn't think the CEO of American Airlines would be sharing an oatmeal breakfast with the CEO of US Airways eight months later. I privately wondered if, at some point, they might graduate from breakfast to a champagne toast.

I had come to expect pithy words of wisdom from Harvey Miller as important milestones unfolded. The Oatmeal Summit provided ample fodder and Harvey did not disappoint: "Missiles launched. We are at Defcon 4."

With the Protocol Agreement in place, and a face-to-face meeting between Horton and Parker behind us, the UCC salivated over the prospect of substantive merger discussions with the Phoenix Bird. We quickly threw cold water on that idea, reminding the UCC that we first needed a nondisclosure agreement ("NDA") with US Airways before any discussions could begin.

I figured the NDA would be relatively easy to negotiate. US Airways had been pestering us about merger discussions for many months and the UCC advisors would strongly consider the sale of their firstborn children in exchange for merger discussions. I saw no reason that we could not wrap up the NDA quickly. I was wrong. The NDA became a lightning rod for strong disagreement.

Before we ever had an opportunity to discuss the substance of the NDA, the UCC advisors pressed for a "side letter" to the Protocol Agreement to address a host of collateral issues important to the UCC. We didn't object to the idea of a side letter, but the kinds of things they demanded were way out of bounds. For example, they wanted us to file the NDA as a Form 8-K with the SEC. An 8-K is a public document that serves as a vehicle to notify shareholders of important events. In this situation, because we hadn't even begun discussions with US Airways, there was no way that the NDA could possibly rise to the level of importance to warrant an 8-K. The UCC's request was a blatant attempt to create additional "buzz" about a possible combination and definitely not rooted in sound legal principle.

They also demanded that we make a public filing (called an HSR filing) with the Federal Trade Commission and the Department of Justice. HSR stands for Hart-Scott-Rodino and refers to a federal law that requires companies to make a premerger notification filing. Again, at this early stage, there was no basis for the filing as there was no pending merger or anything resembling a merger.

And the list went on. The advisors wanted a provision authorizing them to go over our heads and communicate directly with our board if they concluded that the company was not giving the merger a fair and complete review, or if the consolidation discussions were not moving forward with sufficient speed. It was one of those "read my lips" moments—there was no way we would allow the UCC direct access to our board.

The UCC went one step further. They demanded an unfettered voice in the negotiations and the right to speak unilaterally with US Airways' representatives. Not only did we say "hell no," we demanded that the NDA contain a "standstill" agreement that in effect prohibited US Airways from speaking to anyone, including the UCC, during the period of time agreed to in the NDA. The last thing we needed was for the UCC to meddle with US Airways or for Parker's team to conspire with the UCC to formulate a competing plan behind our backs.

The back and forth on the NDA and side letter came down to a single word—control. Just as Harvey Miller feared, Butler and his band of merry men desperately wanted to play kingmaker and they expected everyone to line up like pawns in a game of chess.

In late July, I placed a telephone call to Steve Johnson, my counterpart at US Airways. I was acquainted with Johnson from industry-related meetings and I figured it would be good to let him know where we stood on the NDA. Johnson has a marathon runner physique and Mick Jagger-like hair, along with an insatiable appetite for work.

My conversation with Steve did not go well. I didn't know why, but Steve was not particularly engaging. For a company that seemed hell-bent on merging, I found his tight-lipped demeanor a bit troubling.

Following my conversation with Johnson, I wondered whether the guys in Phoenix were genuinely interested in signing an NDA or if they had other tricks up their sleeves. Meanwhile, once the UCC realized we weren't going to agree to its demands, we made good progress on the side letter. They agreed to back off the demand for the 8-K and HSR filings, and abandoned their request for direct access to our board. In return, we agreed they could attend all joint negotiating sessions with US Airways, but only in the capacity as observers. They could not participate verbally in the negotiations.

With those issues put to bed, Butler demanded that we sign the side letter agreement. We refused, telling him we would sign the letter only if US Airways agreed to sign the NDA. That led to a series of exasperated email messages and phone calls from Butler. It was always the same with him. If we did not do as instructed, he would huff and puff, get red in the face, and threaten a myriad of dire consequences. As Harvey observed, our refusal to sign sent Butler into "suborbital ellipse."

Four days after my initial phone call with Johnson, he called back. Steve apologized for his less than forthcoming demeanor during the earlier conversation, explaining that at the time of my call, he and his team believed that American was not serious about engaging in substantive merger discussions. They were convinced that the draft NDA would be a sham and reflect our lack of enthusiasm. Now that they had finished their review of the document, he said they found it fair and surprisingly complete. He promised that his team would provide comments quickly and hoped that we could sign the NDA without delay.

Hope runs eternal. Back and forth negotiations on the NDA were brutal. I'm glad I didn't calculate the total cost of the NDA negotiations. The attorney's fees likely exceeded one hundred thousand dollars. Too bad we couldn't ask Judge Lane to "reject" legal expenses the same way he rejected labor contracts.

The parties exchanged a multitude of drafts of the NDA, and American and the UCC advisors went 'round and 'round on the side letter to the Protocol Agreement. Someone had to make the agreed upon changes, prepare a red-line draft incorporating the changes, forward revised drafts internally, then forward new agreements to the opposing team. And, of course, we expected the changes to be done correctly at breakneck speed. The Weil associate charged with this task was David Gail, an SMU law graduate who had worked at the firm for four years. Gail was one of those extraordinarily gifted attorneys whose value cannot be estimated. His draftsmanship skills were akin to a superhero's powers. I was thankful he was a member of the team.

On August 30, 2012, American and US Airways publicly announced the signing of mutual nondisclosure agreements. With this hurdle behind us, substantive due diligence discussions between our two companies were finally set to begin. The first meetings were scheduled for the following week in New York City.

Judging by the size of the group assembled, one would think it was a church service on Easter Sunday. We gathered in an enormous conference room at Weil's office overlooking Central Park. There was no seating chart, but intricate rules of seating decorum were in full swing. It was a perfect case study for a sociology professor.

Typically, the seat of power in a business setting is located at the head of a table. But not in this case. With two "opposing" parties and a long rectangular table, each side lined up opposite one another on one of the two long sides of the rectangle. The sweet spot was the center seat on each long side. The worst seats were those on the short sides of the rectangle. Those seats were like Switzerland—neutral and of little importance. As I recall, that's where the UCC observers were forced to sit (and I got a bit of twisted satisfaction watching them shuffle off to their lesser seats). The rule of "power seating" is instinctual for lawyers and bankers, so it was comical to watch the seating dance play out before the meeting started.

Both US Airways and American came prepared with lengthy written presentations that described their respective views of the synergies (additional revenue and cost savings), and the dissynergies (higher costs) of a merger, along with estimated one-time costs. The goal of these initial meetings was to gain an understanding of how each of us valued a potential merger. We needed to know if the two sides were anywhere close to being in the same ballpark.

Synergies in an airline merger take many forms. By far the largest synergy is the incremental passenger revenue derived from a much larger route network. In this case, a merger between American and US Airways would vault American to the enviable position as the world's largest airline. This is one of those times in life where size really does matter. Airline executives tout the advantage of size, believing that larger networks deliver a disproportionate share of business.

That's why you don't see—with few exceptions—two airlines operating connecting hubs at the same airport. Once an airline builds a significant size advantage at an airport, its share of revenues is even larger. It might carry 55 percent of total passengers at a particular airport, but generate 65 percent or more of passenger revenues. So the larger network we have, the better off we are in the markets we serve.

There are also a number of cost synergies in airline mergers. These include operating efficiencies, consolidation of airport and ground facilities (like gates and maintenance bases), and a reduction in the cost of redundant information systems. And, speaking of redundancy, after a merger, companies save employee expenses by shedding duplicate management positions, starting with the CEO, CFO, and general counsel (regrettably), along with significant numbers of managers throughout the organization.

On the other side of the equation, mergers carry a multitude of dis-synergies, including IT integration costs, non-standardized aircraft fleets (interior, exterior and avionics), combining frequent flyer programs, and higher labor costs. To be successful, synergies must far outweigh dis-synergies.

In this instance, one of the big unknowns was the cost of the labor dis-synergy. It was impossible to calculate the true incremental cost of the conditional labor agreements (the CLAs that US Airways negotiated with our labor groups) when measured against American's labor costs because the CLAs were not much more than outlines of what full-fledged agreements might look like. This issue became a huge sticking point in the months that followed.

As potential merger parties spar over the value of synergies, a big stumbling block often centers on the question of "durability." That is, how long do synergies last? If an airline believes they will achieve network revenue gains, will those gains continue for ten years, five years, or some lesser period? Is it fair to assume that competitors will sit back and let the newly merged entity capture market share without reacting? What if there is a merger among other competitors that further alters the competitive landscape? Calculating durability is without question more art than science. Plenty of mergers fail because executives overvalue synergies and underestimate dis-synergies.

To no one's surprise, US Airways' view of synergies was robust, while American's view was more conservative.

US Airways president Scott Kirby led the US Airways due diligence team. Kirby is the kind of guy who quickly ingratiates himself to everyone in the room. He is personable, yet often comes across as a bit arrogant. A 1989 graduate of the Air Force Academy, he fits the mold—physically adept, lean, and smart. He was once described to me as a mathematical savant and I quickly learned that it was close to the truth. He is a whiz with facts and figures.

Kirby and his team came well prepared. The presentation was impressive. It laid out in great detail how a merger would create a much stronger network both in breadth (the number of cities served) and depth (the number of daily flights to a city). Kirby also emphasized that the two networks were highly complementary, not duplicative. For example, American had large hubs in DFW, Miami, and Chicago, along with a large concentration of flights in New York and Los Angeles. US Airways, on the other hand, maintained hubs in Phoenix, Philadelphia, and Charlotte, with a large presence in Washington, D.C.

The networks were also complementary on the international front. American had a vast international network, one grounded in the **one**world alliance, while US Airways—a secondary member of the Star Alliance—had a relatively small international footprint, primarily flying to cities American did not serve. In other words, there was little overlap between the networks of our two airlines.

Kirby cited additional areas of revenue and cost synergies, offset only marginally by cost dis-synergies and one-time costs. By the time he concluded, he managed to assign a value to the deal that ran in excess of a billion dollars annually. Kirby's synergy number was no big surprise. It was consistent with the number he and Parker floated publicly on an April 25, 2012, earnings call with financial analysts.

"Indeed, we estimate that the synergies created by a US-AMR merger—net of the labor dis-synergies we compared against AMR standalone 1113 plan—conservatively are estimated at over 1.2 billion dollars per year," Kirby told analysts.

Not to be outdone, the American presentation was equally impressive. Bev Goulet kicked off the presentation, then turned to Candice Irvin to walk through the bulk of the materials. Irvin was a managing director in American's corporate development department and a veteran of the airline. She is smart, profoundly dedicated, and her knowledge of the airline business runs deep. Irvin has a dry, acerbic wit, and doesn't pull any punches.

In the weeks leading up to this meeting, Goulet and her team worked hard to calculate the value of a US Airways merger. The difficulty, one shared equally by both American and US Airways, is that valuations are only as good as the inputs used to derive the value. Tweaking the inputs leads to a correspondingly higher or lower valuation. In our case, we were careful not to overstate the value of synergies. A significant area of disagreement had to do with durability—how many years the incremental revenue and cost savings would continue.

Both sides acknowledged that most merger synergies decline over time, but there was little agreement regarding the speed of the decline. This was especially important in this deal because we knew that a substantial portion of the synergies would be offset by higher labor costs that were inevitable when long-term labor agreements were negotiated to replace the CLAs. If a significant portion of the synergies failed to materialize, the incremental value of the merger would be lost.

As Irvin wrapped up the presentation, I knew the UCC advisors were displeased. A more appropriate word would be outraged. They quickly accused us of sandbagging the numbers, believing that we did so in an effort to quell enthusiasm for a merger. Likewise, we accused them of prejudging the benefits of a merger without giving serious consideration to the benefits of American emerging from bankruptcy as an independent airline. Our relationship with the advisors was already frayed at the edges. Now, with the merger genie out of the bottle, I feared it would worsen, not improve.

CHAPTER 15

NO TURNING BACK

A mere twenty-four hours after the merger synergy presentation at Weil's office, it became clear that our relationship with the UCC advisors had indeed taken a turn for the worse. I learned that Jack Butler had requested a meeting with Tom Horton to advise him that the UCC had lost confidence in senior management.

It was clear that "senior management" referred to Bev and me. I was pretty sure that the meeting request was a form of payback because she and I refused to bow down to recent UCC demands. After Tom Roberts and Chris Lawrence interceded and agreed to meet with Butler and listen to his concerns, he dropped his request for the Horton meeting.

The lack of trust among the parties was front and center, clouding virtually every conversation, every move we made. Like the Hatfields and McCoys, the level of animus ran deep. The UCC advisors and most of the UCC questioned our motives and saw a conspiracy lurking behind even our most innocuous moves.

The trust quotient with labor was worse still. Whatever modicum of trust we had with labor before 2003 evaporated during that year's crisis and never fully recovered. Arpey made inroads with labor during his 2003-2011 tenure, but ultimately lost their faith and confidence. With Horton now running the company, things were no better. Labor leaders blamed Horton for filing bankruptcy in late 2011 and detested his proposed labor concessions and work rule changes.

By 2012, trust was at an all-time low and so too was labor's loyalty to management. Labor leaders found comfort in the overtures from Doug Parker and his troops. They were anxious to throw AA executives out and anoint Parker king. To make matters worse, we convinced ourselves that the views of labor leaders did not reflect the sentiments of rank and file employees.

Many executives believed that employees across the system would rise up in great numbers in opposition to a merger with US Airways. Bev and I did not share that view. Nonetheless, we waited for the anti-merger revolt. We listened for signs of support from employees across our vast network, but heard none. Whether at airport terminals, on the tarmac, in the cockpit, at maintenance bases, in reservation call centers, or in ramp ready rooms, it was the same thing—nothing. The silence was deafening.

Merger discussions with US Airways continued apace throughout the period of pilot unrest. We were immersed in a fight for the future of our company and our adversaries mounted an offensive from all angles. Dozens of dedicated American employees and outside advisors devoted long hours to advance our agenda. Personal lives and families were sacrificed as we toiled late into the night.

My wife, Michele Valdez, is an attorney and spent several years as in-house counsel at American before taking a position as vice president of the human resources and labor relations department at American Eagle, the company's commuter airline. Like me, Michele is saddled with a Type A personality. She is smart and clever, with old school common sense. I am straitlaced and reserved, while Michele is strong-willed and passionate. We are both strong communicators and share almost everything. In the late 1990s, her career was taking off and so was mine, but with a newly adopted baby and older children to care for, she left the company to take the reins full time at home. A few years later, I became general counsel.

Michele loved being at home, but desperately missed the frenetic pace of the airline business. I often came home from work exhausted, urgently needing a moment, perhaps two, of quiet solitude. Michele greeted me and waited patiently—sort of. She silently counted the minutes, circling like a lioness stalking her prey. When she could wait no longer, the ambush commenced—a multitude of questions about the latest developments at the company.

The topic made no difference to her—labor, bankruptcy, merger—any morsel of information to satisfy her craving to once again be in the thick of combat. Naturally, being a lawyer, she understood my obligations under the attorney-client privilege and my duties of confidentiality. Nevertheless, anything in the public domain was fair game. After I explained the dynamics of a particular problem, she would, without provocation, offer a detailed list of suggested maneuvers to resolve the issue at hand.

Around this same time, mid-September 2012, another player entered the fray, one that would play an important role in the coming months. It was known as the Ad Hoc Group of AMR Corporation Creditors, or the "Ad Hocs" for short. This group had roughly 12 members and held a significant amount of American Airlines debt—collectively, about 1 billion dollars. We considered the Ad Hocs a potential ally, believing they might align themselves with us and counter the agenda of the UCC. Conversely, we knew they might align with an interest contrary to ours. Either way, we needed to keep close tabs on them going forward.

In bankruptcy, few creditors pay their own costs and expenses. Instead, everyone looks to the debtor for reimbursement. The Ad Hocs were no different. The Ad Hocs hired a legal and financial team to assist them in the bankruptcy case and they wanted us to pay for those services. The Ad Hocs hired Milbank Tweed Hadley & McCloy as its legal advisor, and Houlihan Lokey as its investment banker. Milbank Tweed filed a motion with Judge Lane asking that the debtor pay for the services of both companies. Knowing that we needed them on our side, we were not in a position to object and Judge Lane approved the request. We agreed to pay Houlihan 150,000 dollars a month and agreed to pay Milbank its customary hourly fee. It was another one of those "grin and bear it" moments.

By late September, the situation with the APA was at a breaking point. Although Judge Lane's ruling allowed us to throw out the old pilot contract, we now had little prospect of getting a new contract anytime soon. Meanwhile, the pilots seemed content to use the "slowdown" to dismantle the airline's flight schedule.

We had had enough. It was time to go to court and seek an injunction to stop the slowdown. We informed pilot union leaders of our plans and demanded they tell their members to stop the illegal job action. The APA reacted negatively and used a number of choice words to describe management's behavior, including a comparison to bullies, along with a suggestion that our actions were akin to taking a baseball bat to the head. As usual, the union denied there was a slowdown despite clear evidence to the contrary. Nevertheless, the APA sent a message to all pilots asking them to stop disrupting the system, while at the same time blaming the problem on AA's poor maintenance practices.

A few more days passed with no improvement to our operating system. Fearing that a lawsuit would irrevocably damage our relationship with the pilots, Denise Lynn and her team tried one last-ditch effort to resolve the impasse. She told the pilots that we would not implement further changes to pilot work rules if the pilots would return to the bargaining table.

Knowing that union leadership was anxious to resolve the slowdown, our proposal provided the political "cover" they needed with their membership (in times past Jeff Brundage referred to this principle as "cab fare home"). Not surprisingly, shortly after the union announced a resumption of negotiations, the flight system magically "fixed" itself and began a steady climb back to normal. With the pilots back at the negotiating table, we hoped to quickly reach a new agreement and get it ratified.

New York City was quickly becoming my second home. I worried that if I spent much more time there I would owe income taxes to the State of New York. Most of my nights were spent at hotels in Midtown Manhattan, including a Marriott hotel on 57th street. It was conveniently located—a quick ten-minute walk from Weil Gotshal's office. As a debtor in bankruptcy, the AA team remained cognizant of expenses and the hotel was an excellent bargain.

During my thirty years at American, we rarely stayed at expensive hotels so this was no different. The same was true of meal expenses. There was a small, rundown pizza joint just two doors down the street from the hotel. I frequently cajoled my colleagues into grabbing a pizza and beer at the end of a long day. The beer was cold, the pizza hot, and the price couldn't be beat. I'm sorry to say that my pizza place has since closed.

Aside from pizza and beer, I recall a more upscale dinner with Harvey Miller, Tom Roberts, and Steve Karotkin. We met on September 4 at a restaurant in Midtown. It was a small, Italian restaurant with a dark interior. We got a table off to one side. It was quiet and a good place to talk.

I wasn't particularly pleased with the direction of the case, and I knew the three of them were frustrated with me and others at AA. I asked for their unfiltered views of where we stood. They happily complied.

Harvey started off and minced no words: "This case started as a bankruptcy proceeding. You ceded control to the UCC and it's now more of an M&A transaction."

"Harvey, I hardly think the potential US Airways merger has anything to do with ceding control to the UCC," I countered. "We've been down this road before. I don't think we had a choice. What's done is done."

"That's right, there's no turning back," Harvey shot back. "Captain Jack (another of Harvey's favorite names for Jack Butler) got what he wanted. You will lose this battle."

I looked at Roberts. "Do you agree with Harvey?"

"Yes. This isn't going to turn out like you hoped. The deal with US Airways is going to happen. The whole thing is just going to come down to the split between AA and US."

The unqualified statement surprised me. "So that's it. You think it's over."

Roberts leaned in and lowered his voice: "We're going to work this thing every way we can. I'm just saying that I think we need to prepare ourselves for this outcome and get the most value we can. You need to watch your back if you plan to be one of the survivors."

"What I need," I said, "is for the legal and financial advisors to coalesce around a strategy. We all need to be on the same page."

"What does it matter?" Karotkin countered. "You guys rarely follow our advice. You just end up doing whatever you want."

"You devote way too much energy on PR stuff," Harvey interjected. "You should ignore the media and just focus on the bankruptcy case."

I pushed back, "Well, we can't just remain silent and let US Airways and labor control the dialogue. Operating in a vacuum is not an option."

The back and forth continued throughout the course of dinner. With equal measures of frustration among us, it felt good to air our differences. There were few right answers, only challenges. It was late and time to call it quits. Karotkin graciously paid the check and we walked outside. I thanked Steve for dinner, even though I knew I'd see the bill on Weil's next monthly statement.

Contract negotiations with the APA were now in full swing, but time was not on our side. The US Airways discussions had progressed to an advanced stage and the prospect of convincing our pilots to ratify a new contract became more difficult each day. The APA's governance structure, with authority divided among its national officers, its board of directors, and its negotiating committee, complicated its ability to reach a new tentative agreement with management. It was maddening to witness the dysfunctional process play out among smart, professional people.

Discussions with US Airways continued at a rapid pace throughout the balance of September and October 2012. November promised to be a pivotal month. Most AA executives remained firm in their opposition to a merger, but acknowledged that at the right economic split a deal might make sense.

Even though it was too early to know if a deal would come together, we decided it was prudent to begin work on the principal merger documents so that we would be ready to go on short notice. Glenn West, the managing partner of Weil's Dallas office, was an experienced M&A attorney and assumed responsibility for assembling a draft of the documents. Merger agreements are long and complicated, and contain a myriad of arcane, yet important, provisions. They can be hundreds of pages long. I was glad that Glenn would be the one negotiating these agreements with US Airway's outside counsel, and responsible for explaining it all to the American board, if it came to that.

If, in fact, the two companies merged, there remained a singular belief among most employees inside the American Airlines headquarters—the AA executive management team would run the newly combined company. American was nearly twice the size of US Airways, with more employees, more aircraft, a larger route system, and a vastly superior frequent flyer program. And perhaps most telling, aviation experts consistently touted American's rich history of having the best and brightest management teams in the business.

There was no reason to believe that anyone other than American's team would run the combined airline.

CHAPTER 16

JUDGMENT DAY

I found myself trapped inside what felt like a giant funnel. A funnel filled with disparate interests, swirling and colliding, as they gained momentum on their way down the ever-narrowing spout. I anguished, not knowing what awaited my colleagues and me on the other end of the funnel.

After eight grueling weeks of due diligence discussions, it was time for US Airways to show its hand. Neither side relished the prospect of additional meetings without first knowing if there was a reasonable basis for a deal. A genuine offer from US Airways would do just that. I called Steve Johnson in mid-October and asked when we could expect to see an offer. He responded saying we would receive an offer no later than November 3, 2012. I was pleased that we would soon see what US Airways had in mind.

While we waited for the offer, we scheduled a meeting in Dallas with the UCC advisors to iron out our differences on merger valuation. The meeting was set for October 30, but our timing was lousy. Hurricane Sandy came ashore the previous day, with devastating consequences for the East Coast. For American, it meant massive numbers of flight cancellations, followed by more disruption as the airline repositioned aircraft and accommodated thousands of passengers affected by the storm. Getting the airline back on schedule was a herculean effort.

As a result of Hurricane Sandy, most of the advisors remained grounded on the East Coast and were forced to participate in the meeting by conference call. One of the people most affected by the storm was Steve Karotkin. The powerful storm knocked out all electrical power at his home, and it was not restored for weeks. Steve, along with his caustic sense of humor, never missed a beat. He continued nonstop work on the case, peppering our conversations with a series of one-liners.

As promised, Parker called Horton on November 2 and presented the offer. The proposal was straightforward. It contemplated that American's stakeholders (creditors) would receive 70 percent of the equity in a new, merged company and US Airways shareholders would receive 30 percent of the combined company's equity.

The noneconomic terms (referred to as the social issues or governance issues) were largely favorable to American. The proposal called for AA's headquarters to remain in Fort Worth and the combined company would retain the AA brand name. It also contemplated an eleven-person board, with five members appointed by US Airways and six by American's creditors. But there was one provision that we found particularly troubling—Tom Horton would be out and Doug Parker would be named chairman and CEO of the new company.

We quickly assembled our board on a telephone call to review the terms of the offer. They were not enamored with the notion of merging with US Airways. The Phoenix-based airline had a sizable amount of debt and an unsettled labor dynamic. Their 2005 merger with America West only exacerbated their labor difficulties. Despite the passage of seven years, Parker and his executive team had been unable to integrate the work forces of the two airlines. We found it odd that AA's labor force was bent on merging with a company that had been unable to get its own labor house in order. It seemed to us that it didn't bode well of US Airways' ability to successfully integrate American's labor force with a still-fractured US Airways labor force.

Horton walked the board through the principal elements of Parker's offer. They had several questions but knew we planned a thorough review of the offer at an in-person meeting scheduled eight days later on November 10. For the time being, the board concluded that the economic terms of the offer (the 70/30 equity split) were insufficient, but agreed with Horton that we should continue discussing a possible combination. As to the social issues, they suggested we put them aside for resolution at a later date.

I arrived in New York on Wednesday, November 7, 2012, and planned to camp out at Weil's offices for a full week. I had a busy agenda—meetings were scheduled with the UCC advisors, US Airways, and the Ad Hocs. In addition, we had a lot of work to do in advance of the board meeting set for Saturday. Tom Roberts and I had to prepare a PowerPoint presentation covering legal issues, while Bev Goulet and her team worked on a lengthy synergy presentation.

During the week, Tom Roberts met with Armando Codina, the lead director of our board. Codina, and the full board for that matter, had come to rely on Roberts for advice as questions surfaced regarding a raft of merger-related issues. They held Roberts in high regard. Tom Roberts was a calming presence with his absentminded professor kind of style. He used it to answer the board's questions and quiet their nerves during stressful times.

It was an interesting dynamic. Tom and other Weil attorneys actually served as legal counsel to the company, not the board. Often, a board will hire independent counsel rather than relying on advice from counsel to the company. There is no hard and fast rule about when, or under what circumstances, a board should retain independent counsel. Some boards keep independent counsel on retainer at all times. Others choose to hire counsel only during periods of extreme corporate stress.

During my time as general counsel, the board elected to hire independent counsel on two occasions. The first time arose shortly after Carty resigned from the company in 2003 and Arpey assumed the CEO role. The company was in dire straits and the board hired counsel to examine our governance practices and to assist the board during that difficult period.

I was none too pleased about their decision to hire independent counsel. Even though I was new to the job, I didn't want someone looking over my shoulder, second-guessing my advice. To make matters worse, the board hired Marty Lipton of Wachtell, Lipton, Rosen & Katz. The law firm, and Marty Lipton in particular, are legendary in legal circles. Lipton is a founding member of the firm and specializes in corporate takeovers and representing boards during times of crisis. Lipton arrived on the scene with enormous cachet, and I was concerned that he might attempt to justify his presence by taking the board down a bunch of rabbit holes. My fears were unfounded. Lipton and his team proved helpful and supportive.

The second occasion arose during the 2008 recession. In that situation, the directors decided to hire independent counsel to provide advice on an ongoing basis. On that occasion, the board turned to a lawyer from one of the big Los Angeles-based firms. The assignment didn't last long. They concluded that the arrangement wasn't particularly helpful and ended the relationship several months later.

As I became more comfortable in my role, I realized that independent counsel posed no threat to me as general counsel. Instead, it turned out that counsel to the board was a useful resource in difficult times. As the board got to know me better, I earned their trust and they grew to appreciate and rely on my legal recommendations and advice.

When Roberts or other Weil attorneys met privately with a board member, or with the full board in executive session, Weil assumed a role best described as quasi-independent counsel and provided legal advice without the necessity of hiring independent counsel. The arrangement was, I believe, a testament to the confidence the board placed in me as general counsel, and the level of comfort and trust that existed between the Weil attorneys and the board.

I spent so much time at Weil's New York office that I was provided an entry badge that allowed me to bypass the visitor check-in desk in the main lobby. I looked just like the rest of the dark blue suits heading to the office. The firm occupies multiple floors in the General Motors building on 5th Avenue overlooking Central Park. The Apple store, with its winding staircase to the below-grade entry, is in the same plaza as Weil's office, as was the famous FAO Schwarz toy store. I would often duck into the store to purchase various stuffed animals for my youngest daughter. The guilt of being away from home weighed heavily on me, but as long as I kept the stuffed animals coming, my daughter didn't complain much. My wife, on the other hand, was another story.

We had lunch or an afternoon snack in the Weil cafeteria almost every day. Roberts' legal skills aside, he had the charm of a Texas politician wrapped up in an infectious combination of self-deprecating humor and hijinks. He excelled in the art of harmless banter and used it to greet and make new friends. In today's world of political correctness, he was slightly AWOL, but always managed to endear himself to even the most cynical or salty.

Tom knew the cafeteria workers by name. With a grin and a slight drawl, he inquired of the server at the entree station, "Hey, darlin', what's cookin' today?" To the cashier, an elderly woman who was a staple behind the register, he repeated the same worn-out line, "Does your husband know about us yet? It's our little secret, let's keep it that way." Right on cue, she smiled and gave the same sassy response each time, "I told him, but he don't believe it."

On November 9, we met with the Ad Hocs. We told them that a deal with US Airways, on the right economic terms, could create meaningful value for shareholders. We also teed up the question everyone was talking about, the question of governance—who should run the merged airline? They listened but provided little guidance.

Afterward, I asked Steve Karotkin about the governance issue. "What about the Ad Hocs? They must care who ends up running the business."

Karotkin didn't miss a beat: "No, they don't. The Ad Hocs care about one thing only—money. As long as the deal yields the best financial outcome for them, nothing else matters."

I didn't respond. Sensing my concern, Karotkin took a long breath as the seconds passed, then continued, "Hey, did you hear the one about the rabbi, the Catholic priest, and the lawyer. The three of them are stuck on a deserted island..."

I had a pretty good idea where he was headed. Nevertheless, I was intrigued and already laughing before he delivered the punch line. Sure enough, it was funny, even if it was slightly off-color.

The following day, Saturday, November 10, we met with our board at Weil's office. Bev Goulet reviewed with them our estimates of revenue and cost synergies, dis-synergies, and one-time merger costs. Goulet always carried the burden of presenting massive numbers of PowerPoint slides, with head-hurting economic analyses. Despite the complexity of her presentations, Bev never faltered as she tried to make the incomprehensible understandable to the rest of us mortals. During the meeting, we also had an in-depth discussion regarding labor costs and the status of discussions with the APA. The board was deeply concerned about labor costs.

At the conclusion of the meeting, we knew precisely where the board stood. First, the board told us the 70/30 equity split was unacceptable. They wanted 80/20. Second, the board directed us to inform Parker that he must mitigate labor cost exposure, meaning that he had to convince both companies' unions to sign definitive labor agreements. The so-called "conditional labor agreements" (CLAs) signed months earlier were inadequate. The benefits of a merger could be wiped out by runaway labor costs. If Parker couldn't deliver, there was no way American's board would throw its support in favor of a deal.

The board's demand for an improved split, along with definitive labor agreements, made for a tall order. Harvey Miller stepped in with sage advice: "Stay cool, the game is on."

Two days later, the American team met all day with US Airways and the UCC advisors. The meeting focused on how to achieve the level of labor cost certainty demanded by the AA board. It would be an enormous undertaking to craft definitive labor agreements among so many different union groups at the two companies. Kirby insisted that the CLAs, as written, were a sufficient "fence" around labor costs. We pushed back, arguing that the CLAs weren't worth the paper they were written on. We made little progress that day.

At the end of the day, Bev Goulet and I packed up and headed in the direction of our hotel. I hoped to convince her that pizza and beer would make for a fine way to end the evening. As we walked and discussed events of the day, we heard someone behind us yelling our names. It was Scott Kirby. We turned around and walked towards him.

"Hey, guys, a bunch of us are having drinks and dinner. Why don't you join us?" Bev and I were equally surprised by the invitation. We quickly declined dinner, but agreed to stop in for a beer.

Kirby's invitation to join him, Doug Parker, and the rest of their team for a drink was vintage Kirby. He was a bit of an oddball. He could be terribly confrontational during negotiations, yet always friendly. I knew his invitation for drinks was genuine and that he had no ulterior motive. He was just being himself.

The US Airways team was tucked away in a private room and they welcomed us to the gathering. It was a good-sized group and I took note of their camaraderie. After a drink and sharing a few funny stories, we said our goodbyes and let them get on with dinner.

As Bev and I walked to the hotel, we both agreed that we enjoyed the evening, almost as if the admission was a betrayal to American. If the tables had been reversed, I'm pretty sure the AA people would never extend a similar invitation. It's not that we were unfriendly; we just weren't much fun. It wasn't part of the American Airlines straitlaced DNA.

The Wednesday following the board meeting was my eighth consecutive day in New York. After informing the UCC about our demand for an 80/20 split, we delivered the same news to US Airways. They were angry and immediately threatened to walk the deal. The next day, November 15, the US Airways team met with its board. As expected, they found our proposed equity split unacceptable and claimed they were withdrawing from further negotiations. I didn't believe it for a second. It was classic gamesmanship. They were bluffing and everyone knew it.

Contemporaneous with the game of cat and mouse, we continued to apply pressure on the APA, hoping to strike a deal. We used every point of leverage available. One lever we continued to press concerned a grant of equity to pilots. We promised to give pilots a substantial amount of equity in the newly reorganized company. We estimated that the value of the equity promised, 13.5 percent of our stock, would be worth a whopping 1 billion dollars, to be shared among all pilots. We made similar promises of equity to the APFA and the TWU, albeit in substantially lesser amounts.

I don't know if it was the promise of equity or some other external pressure, but the APA board of directors finally agreed to put a revised tentative agreement in the hands of its membership for ratification. Results of the vote were due December 7, 2012.

This was our last chance with the pilots. It was now or never. I suppose the gods of labor were smiling from the heavens and feeling charitable. Whatever the reason, the union reported that 73.8 percent of its members voted to approve the new contract. With the flight attendant and TWU deals already in the bag, we finally had fully ratified labor contracts with every union at American Airlines. It felt good to bask in the glory of the moment.

With new labor contracts in place at American, we turned our attention to the task of figuring out how to put a "fence" around labor costs of a merged company. In early December, 2012, Denise Lynn, Steve Karotkin, and I had dinner with Kirby and Butler, along with several others, to map out a strategy. We decided to start with the pilots from both airlines in an effort to get them to sign a binding memorandum of understanding (MOU). Personally, I was loath to be immersed directly in discussions with the pilots. I didn't enjoy labor negotiations and I already had my fill dealing with their demands, the slowdown that damaged our operations, the mediation with Judge Peck, and the contentious 1113 proceeding. I gladly let Denise take the lead. I was there principally to keep Kirby and Butler in check.

There were four parties at the bargaining table—American Airlines, US Airways, the APA (representing AA pilots), and the US Airline Pilots Association ("USAPA"), representing US Airways pilots. We also allowed the UCC advisors to participate in the discussions. Our collective goal was to reconcile the terms of the conditional labor agreement signed by US Airways and the APA, with the terms of the new collective bargaining agreement between AA and the APA, while at the same time convincing the APA and USAPA to agree to the terms of a four-party MOU. We also hoped to secure similar letter agreements from American's flight attendant union and the TWU. While our goal was clear, balancing competing interests made for tricky negotiations.

Given the substantial task that lie ahead, all parties agreed that it was important that American and US Airways negotiate as a team to avoid getting crosswise with one another or with the unions. We didn't want American or US Airways representatives to have private sidebar conversations. To accomplish this, both the AA and US Airways teams agreed to adhere strictly to the terms of the longstanding nondisclosure agreement. This meant that no one was authorized to speak unilaterally to the unions.

One day during the negotiations, Denise Lynn and I returned from lunch and saw Kirby speaking with one of the union leaders. It appeared to be a unilateral conversation prohibited by the oral agreement we reached before the negotiations started. Denise and I were livid. We immediately pulled Kirby aside and asked him what the hell he was up to. Rather than giving us some song and dance, he confessed that he had lunch with Laura Glading, president of the American flight attendants' union. He also admitted that he had at least two other meetings with union leaders. We both appreciated his candor, but couldn't believe that he openly violated our agreement prohibiting private conversations with union officials.

"What happened to our agreement not to speak unilaterally to the unions?" we asked. "Your discussions directly violate the terms of the NDA."

He apologized profusely, said he knew it was wrong, but had the conversations anyway because he believed they would prove helpful to both American and US Airways. Denise didn't buy his apology or his reasoning and she let him have it right between the eyes: "Scott, you and I do not share the same value system. We operate under a different set of ethical principles."

Kirby's failure to adhere to the terms of the NDA did not come as a surprise. There were endless leaks of information and violations of nondisclosure obligations by many participants. The situation got so bad that Horton demanded that we file a lawsuit to staunch the improper flow of information. The leaks were frustrating, but I concluded that a lawsuit focused on NDA violations would not advance the ball. If we filed a lawsuit it would take too long to work its way through the court system, and if we won, then what? A victory would not really change anything. It was a losing proposition; Horton reluctantly agreed.

While the negotiations dragged on, one person I intended to meet with was Harvey Miller. During the previous weeks, I had heard little from Harvey. We spoke by phone infrequently, he did not participate in our weekly status discussions, and his pithy emails had all but disappeared. Sensing something was wrong, I picked up the phone and called him. I asked Harvey what was going on. It was a short conversation. He told me that his continued work on the case was a distraction, that we did not value his advice, and that he disagreed with the strategy we had adopted. Sadly, I knew Harvey's assessment was accurate, but told him we would talk further the next time I was in New York.

I kept my word, and one afternoon in between meetings at Weil Gotshal, I took the elevator to Harvey's office on the 29th floor. I'm not exactly sure how the relationship got off track, but I missed his involvement. Harvey combined a brilliant mind, an elegant presentation style, and a caustic wit that made him one of a kind. He always wore stylish clothing and reminded me of an older version of James Bond. His door was open and I walked in.

Harvey greeted me with his customary warm handshake and smile. He asked me to sit and immediately wanted to know how things were proceeding. I spent several minutes bringing him up to date. He asked a number of questions, but offered no advice. We both understood, without saying it, that he had no intention of continuing work on the case. I promised to stop by whenever I was in New York. We shook hands and I left his office. Harvey's departure from the case was a casualty that stuck with me a long time. I regret the way things worked out, but realized there was nothing I could do to change the outcome.

Negotiations with APA and USAPA moved along at a glacial pace. At times, it was difficult to discern if any progress was being made. The four-party talks continued throughout December 2012. The largest sticking point with labor centered on our efforts to expand what is known as the pilot "scope clause." Every pilot labor agreement has a scope clause and it is often the single most important issue to both pilots and management.

For decades, scope clauses simply stated that pilots employed by that airline must perform all flying done by that airline. But, as the airline business grew and regional airlines popped up, major airlines looked for ways to allow pilots from these regional carriers to fly on their behalf. Sometimes, major airlines would enter into a contract with a regional airline, while in other cases the major airline owned the regional carrier. For example, American Airlines owns and operates Envoy Airlines, formerly known as American Eagle Airlines. As it was, American Eagle Airlines was made up of several formerly independent airlines that we later purchased.

As regional flying increased, unions at the mainline carriers, like American, demanded strict limits to the size and number of aircraft that could be flown by regional carriers. Mainline pilots blame broad scope clauses for the loss of pilot jobs to regional carriers, and management complains that narrow scope clauses impede their ability to compete. The conflicting interests of the company and pilots became a decades old tug of war. Scope clauses went from being a single paragraph in the collective bargaining agreement to its own multipage supplement.

Initially, scope issues focused on aircraft with less than thirty-five seats. Then it was over the introduction of regional jets of up to fifty seats, then seventy seats. With the advent of larger regional aircraft with eighty to one hundred seats, major carriers continue to push the limits of scope and pilot unions continue to push back.

The scope negotiations with APA and USAPA were long and complicated. Each carrier's scope clauses contained different limitations, in part because the carriers flew different regional aircraft.

Discussing scope is akin to discussing politics at a Sunday family dinner—a topic to be avoided at all costs. The four-party scope negotiations had the same feel. The negotiations were heated and tempers flared. Jack Butler and I went at each other with great intensity when he accused American of being inflexible with regard to scope generally, and a new aircraft type, the Embraer 190, a new one hundred-seat aircraft, in particular. Butler has a size advantage, but I figured my agility might level the playing field if the argument turned physical. Fortunately, harsh words intermingled with profanity proved a sufficient elixir to fisticuffs.

The labor negotiating teams continued to meet in earnest over the holiday break, with Denise Lynn leading the charge for American. Eventually, they hammered out a suitable compromise on scope and were able to work through the remaining issues dividing the parties. Perhaps the teams were battle-fatigued, or maybe it was good holiday cheer. It didn't really matter. The four parties—AA, US Airways, APA and USAPA—crossed the finish line on December 29 and signed a binding memorandum of agreement.

With the pilot MOU completed, the negotiating teams turned their attention to the TWU and the APFA. By the end of January 2013, American, US Airways and the TWU signed a three-party memorandum of agreement. The flight attendants from both companies took a slightly different path but achieved similar results. US Airways signed a new collective bargaining agreement with its flight attendants (the Association of Flight Attendants) and signed a letter agreement with the APFA. Both of those agreements cited support for the merger.

The signing of these agreements was a significant turning point in the march toward a merger of the two airlines. Ever since merger speculation began shortly after our November 29, 2011, bankruptcy filing, labor was always the wild card in the deck. Now, with labor agreements under our belt, the wild card was no longer an unknown quantity. Admittedly, the agreements were only the first step in the process. If the merger went forward, the new company would still need to negotiate full CBAs with each union, and those negotiations could easily lead to new and costly demands from labor.

Nevertheless, the agreements accomplished exactly what the AA board requested—they mitigated potential labor risks and substantially reduced labor cost uncertainty.

As January 2013 arrived, the merger funnel narrowed precipitously. For me, the prospect of a merger with US Airways was no longer a possibility or a probability—it was a certainty. There were lots of important issues yet to be resolved, but in my mind a merger was no longer a question of "if," just a question of how long it would take to resolve the open issues.

This "merger certainty" became ever more real following a meeting with the Ad Hocs on January 15. We invited the Ad Hocs to Fort Worth to discuss their views regarding the proposed merger. It was no accident that the meeting date happened to coincide with the delivery of a new 777-300 from Boeing just days earlier. The aircraft was housed temporarily in a hangar at DFW Airport. We took the Ad Hocs to the hangar to show off the new plane and used the time to impress upon them that American Airlines was moving forward and headed in the right direction.

That same day, we listened to the Ad Hocs describe their conclusions regarding the enterprise value of American Airlines as an independent carrier, compared to the enterprise value of the company if we merged with US Airways. Their assessment of the two alternatives was clear and straightforward—hands down they favored a merger of the two airlines, in large part because they concluded that a merger would maximize the recovery to creditors.

On this point—the recovery to creditors—we were in total agreement with the Ad Hocs. Horton and Goulet, along with our financial advisors at Rothschild, all concluded that a combination of the two airlines would provide the best economic outcome for American's creditors. They also concluded that, at the right equity split, unsecured creditors would be paid in full and existing shareholders would receive a substantial distribution, something that rarely occurs in bankruptcy. US Airways' latest offer called for a 70/30 equity split and American's counteroffer stood at 80/20. It was a large gap, one that would not be resolved easily.

The other looming question, the real elephant in the room, needed to be addressed: Who would who run the combined company—Doug Parker or Tom Horton? Like lobbyists at a Washington, D.C., soiree, various parties began making the pitch for their preferred choice. Some parties' allegiance was easy to discern. American's labor leaders made their positions known early. They wanted Horton and the rest of his team out and Parker and his team in. There were a few labor stalwarts who felt otherwise and promised to rally the troops in favor of a Horton-led management team. We waited for those promises to materialize into something tangible, but we never saw evidence of that support.

For a brief period of time, the UCC advisors pretended to be noncommittal and listened as we laid out the reasons why Horton should be CEO of the combined company. On its face, American was by far the larger of the two companies and even at a 70/30 split, our constituencies would end up owning the bulk of the company. What's more, American had a more complex and far-flung footprint than US Airways, particularly in international markets. Horton was chairman of the oneworld alliance and he carried substantial influence with our partners across the globe. All of this pointed to Horton as the logical choice as CEO. Despite the rationale, the UCC advisors abandoned any pretext of being noncommittal and lined up in support of Parker as the heir apparent. It was a stinging blow.

On the other side of the spectrum, the vast majority of management employees couldn't begin to entertain the notion that Horton might not be CEO. Such an outcome was simply inconceivable and evoked a visceral reaction, one grounded in devotion to the airline and a belief that American's management team was the best in the business. For them, it bordered on heresy for anyone in the company to think otherwise.

The officer core at American shared these sentiments and desperately wanted to do something to stem the rising tide in favor of Parker. Almost daily, officers stopped by my office bewildered by the prospect that Parker might end up as CEO. I'm sure many of my colleagues secretly wondered whether those of us running the bankruptcy and merger discussions had just plain screwed up. They left my office dejected and bewildered.

One vice president felt compelled to take some kind of action so he drafted a letter in support of Horton as CEO and convinced all vice presidents to sign the letter. This officer was a friend. I helped him get his job at American and our families had spent time together on social occasions. He was smart but sometimes headstrong to a fault. He wanted to send the letter to our board of directors and asked for my permission to do so. Given the state of discussions with the UCC and others on this topic, I explained that such a letter would appear self-serving and only complicate matters. The letter was a nice gesture, but a bad idea.

My directive led to a series of harsh phone calls and heated in-person discussions. This episode was representative of the passion and emotional upheaval that management experienced as these events unfolded.

The final constituency holding sway on the issue was the Ad Hoc committee of creditors. We knew their opinion carried significant weight and we lobbied hard to convince them that we were the better team. But I recalled Karotkin's admonition months earlier about the Ad Hocs—the only thing they really care about is money. They gave lip service to what we had to say, but it soon became clear they weren't going to fall on a sword or any other sharp instrument concerning governance of a combined company. It made no difference to them one way or another.

As January rolled along, the merger between American and US Airways continued to gain momentum. While the horse had not yet left the barn, the barn doors were beginning to swing open. The signs were everywhere. Among those signs—Horton and Parker met on multiple occasions to discuss the equity split and governance issues, and the boards of both companies received ever more frequent updates. A pivotal sign occurred on January 27. On that day, our lead director Armando Codina met face-to-face with Doug Parker to discuss the merger.

Codina went to the meeting armed with three demands from the AMR board: First, he told Parker that the 70/30 equity split was insufficient and must be improved. Second, he explained that the management structure of the new company must be one that maximized the likelihood of achieving the expected merger synergies, and that AMR's stakeholders must select more members of the new board than originally proposed by US Airways.

The third and final demand was of paramount importance to Horton and the AMR board. Codina told Parker that existing AMR equity holders must receive an economic recovery in the Chapter 11 case. In most bankruptcy cases, equity holders receive nothing and their equity is wiped clean. But in this case, the combined enterprise value of the two companies had enormous value, and the board demanded that equity holders share in the spoils.

On January 30, Bev Goulet and I received a curious invitation. Scott Kirby asked both of us to meet him for breakfast at the Crescent Hotel in Dallas. I wasn't sure what Kirby had up his sleeve and I was anxious to find out. After we were seated, he got right to the point. He told us that the merger was a foregone conclusion. I agreed, but remained silent. He said that both of us were well-liked by the US Airways team and that Parker wanted both of us to work for the new company. Kirby asked what jobs we might be interested in.

I wrestled with my response. We still had a tough set of negotiations in front of us and the conversation seemed premature. Nevertheless, I told him the only job I wanted was the general counsel job and that I had one condition. I told him that I had always reported directly to the CEO and that I would demand the same reporting structure going forward. Kirby listened but made no commitment.

Back and forth negotiations continued around the clock into February. The discussions remained heated, as Horton continued to push for a greater equity split for American's creditors. After much consideration, US Airways upped the ante to 72/28. With the increased equity split, American's board agreed to the improved terms, provided that US Airways assumed any liability for certain employee postretirement benefits.

On the governance issue, it was clear that Parker would be CEO. He had all the leverage. The only party that could have made a difference was the Ad Hocs and they chose to remain silent. However, Horton and Parker agreed that Horton would serve as chairman of the board of the combined company for one year or until the next annual meeting of shareholders, whichever occurred first.

The final big issue—a recovery for equity holders—worked out better than anyone could have expected. Following lengthy negotiations with the Ad Hocs and in large part due to the insistence of Horton, Codina and the rest of the board, 3.5 percent of the combined company's equity was allocated to AMR's existing shareholders. This meant that equity holders would receive stock valued in the hundreds of millions, if not billions, of dollars, an unheard-of result. With those final additions, the two boards voted to approve the merger on the evening of February 13.

The deal was done. Fourteen months after American Airlines filed for bankruptcy, we now stood side by side with US Airways—on Valentine's Day, February 14, 2013—and announced the planned merger of our two airlines. The combination would return American to the position it held for many years. It would once again be the world's largest airline.

The announcement was big news. For some, it represented the culmination of a dream come true. For others, the excitement was tempered by unease about what lie ahead. Either way, I figured my troubles were behind me. We still needed regulatory approval of the merger, but that looked to be an easy task. I figured wrong.

CHAPTER 17

PARTY CRASHERS

In the days following the merger announcement, the frenetic pace of the previous two years was replaced by a strange sense of calm. To be sure, we faced a daunting array of tasks to complete the merger and exit from bankruptcy, but the path was no longer littered with warring factions or competing interests. Everyone, it seemed, was on the same page and knew exactly what needed to be done.

Parker's army rolled into American's headquarters like a swarm of locusts invading a field of crops. This would soon be their new home and they wasted no time settling in. I wondered which of the US Airways executives were destined to become permanent residents and which of the American team would be asked to vacate the premises. Such is the prerogative of the conquering army.

Doug Parker faced an important decision, one that required an equal mix of leadership and diplomacy—the selection of the new American Airlines executive team.

During merger negotiations, Parker and Horton considered a variety of ways to figure out who would stay and who would go. As outgoing CEO, Horton wanted equal say in the selection process. Parker balked at the idea, arguing that as CEO, he would be held accountable for the success of the combined airline and needed full discretion to hire whomever he deemed most suitable. In the end, it was agreed that Parker would choose among the "best of the best" from the American and US Airways management teams, with input and advice from Horton.

Rumor about Parker's hiring plans ran amok. Would Parker pick and choose among executives from both airlines, or simply install the US Airways team en masse? Careers and futures hung in the balance. As his selections would have far-reaching "trickle-down" effects throughout the organization, all eyes were on Parker, watching and waiting to see what he would do.

While Parker contemplated the makeup of his executive team, I focused my efforts on two critical matters—bankruptcy court approval of our plan of reorganization and government approval of the merger.

We walked through the doors of the bankruptcy court on November 29, 2011. Now, some fifteen months later, we were headed to the exit doors, anxious to leave the world of bankruptcy behind us. The exit process is not easy. It is complicated and tedious.

To emerge from bankruptcy, the law requires a debtor to present a plan of reorganization to the court and to its creditors for approval. Each creditor claim is placed into a separate class (for instance, general unsecured creditors are in one class and secured creditors are in another class) and each creditor in the class has the opportunity to vote to either accept or reject the debtor's plan. At least half of the creditors in each class, representing at least two-thirds of the total value of claims in the class, must vote in favor of the plan. If a class of creditors does not approve the plan, there are "cramdown" provisions in the bankruptcy code that enable the debtor, under certain conditions, to force unhappy creditors to accept its plan.

It was one of those times when having bankruptcy lawyers with a wealth of experience is worth every bit of the high-priced fees these lawyers demand. I looked to Steve Karotkin, Alfredo Perez, and Steve Youngman, along with a cadre of Weil associates and paralegals, to stickhandle the effort. I was thankful that I was preoccupied with other matters because I had no desire to get in the middle of intricate bankruptcy rules and procedures. They didn't say as much, but I know the Weil lawyers were happy that I didn't meddle in their affairs.

Unlike the minutiae of bankruptcy laws that I managed to delegate to the Weil attorneys (and several attorneys from my staff), I was deeply immersed in the effort to secure government approval of our planned merger. The way the antitrust rules work, companies seeking to merge don't actually receive approval or disapproval from the Department of Justice. Instead, if the government concludes that a proposed merger is anticompetitive, it will file a lawsuit to enjoin the transaction. On the other hand, the DOJ will take no action if it concludes that a proposed merger is permissible. Typically, if it elects to stand down, it does so after exacting concessions from the merging parties as a condition of its decision not to block the deal.

A close look at recent airline mergers gave us tremendous confidence that Justice would not attempt to block the American/US Airways merger. In 2008, the merger between No. 3 Delta Air Lines and No. 4 Northwest Airlines sailed easily through DOJ, requiring only small concessions from the two airlines. The combination of Delta and Northwest was a notable event, especially inside American's headquarters building. The newly merged Delta surpassed American as the world's largest airline.

Two years later, United Airlines and Continental Airlines signed an agreement to merge their airlines. Once again, the DOJ did not sue to block that transaction after United agreed to surrender a number of gates and slots at crowded Newark Liberty International Airport. With this merger, United eclipsed Delta as the world's largest carrier and American slipped to third place.

Rounding out the merger picture, in May 2011, the leading U.S. low-fare carrier, Southwest Airlines, merged with another low-fare airline, AirTran Airways. Again, DOJ did not contest that merger.

After those mergers, American was the third largest carrier and US Airways was the fifth largest. If we combined, the new American would again catapult to the top of the heap.

On its face, a merger with US Airways looked like a slam dunk. The route networks of the two carriers were highly complementary. There were very few nonstop domestic overlapping markets. The same was true on the international front. The number of overlapping markets is a big deal to the DOJ when it comes time to analyze the competitive effects of a merger. Having so few overlaps with US Airways really buttressed our confidence that DOJ would not object to the deal.

Given that Justice approved three airline mergers within the previous five years, I felt confident that we should have a relatively easy time achieving regulatory clearance for the AA/US Airways merger. On several occasions, and long before we filed for bankruptcy in November 2011, we discussed potential merger partners with our board of directors. On each of those occasions, I shared my prediction that achieving DOJ "approval" of a merger with US Airways would be a walk in the park. We knew that the DOJ would force us to divest slots and gates at Washington Reagan, maybe even New York LaGuardia, but we believed we could get this deal done, unless...

"Here's the problem. We're the caboose—the last of the big airline mergers. I'm not sure Justice is going to let this one go through. Because after this, consolidation in the industry is basically finished."

I was in a meeting with outside counsel about the prospect of the DOJ objecting to the proposed merger. The person speaking was MJ Moltenbrey, a former Justice Department lawyer and currently a partner in the antitrust division at Paul Hastings in Washington, D.C. Working at the DOJ tends to elevate a lawyer in the eyes of their peers. A Justice Department "alum" knows the inside workings and personalities of the department and we hoped to leverage that knowledge to our advantage. MJ was not one of those ego-driven lawyers who loved to hear themselves speak. She was typically soft-spoken, so I listened carefully whenever she provided advice because it was always savvy and on point. We hired her firm, along with a cadre of others, to help us secure government approval of the merger. MJ was responding to a question I posed to her and Joe Sims.

Joe Sims was one of the country's foremost antitrust lawyers and a senior partner at Jones Day, a huge multinational law firm with over 2,500 lawyers. Bald, sixty-five-plus years of age, with a gravelly voice, Joe is a straight-talking, take-no-prisoners kind of guy who says what he means.

"Joe, do you agree with MJ?" I asked. "Is Justice going to oppose this deal?"

"Look, we have no idea what's in US Airways' documents," he replied. "There could be all kinds of bad stuff. We just don't know. Until we see them, we're in the dark. I've seen a bunch of deals crater because people say stupid things."

Listening to Joe and MJ made me wonder whether my prediction to the board that DOJ clearance of the merger would be a "walk in the park" might turn out to be a slog through the mud.

Shortly after we signed the merger agreement in February 2013, the DOJ sent both American and US Airways a request for documents. A request to produce documents is typical in these kinds of cases. And true to form, the request was broad and deep. The DOJ wanted to look at every document, every email, and every scrap of paper that might shed some light on the competitive implications of the proposed merger. DOJ lawyers and economists pored over these documents in an effort to determine if the merger would be anticompetitive and harmful to consumers. In our case, they mostly wanted to know if the merger would result in higher airfares to consumers.

As soon as we received the document request, both American and US Airways began assembling the materials requested by Justice. For those who have never experienced a document production in a major regulatory matter, it is a nightmare of a project. Unlike years ago when documents consisted mostly of written correspondence and file folders stuffed into cabinet drawers, today the vast majority of documents are electronic—emails, PowerPoint presentations, Word documents and Excel spreadsheets.

During my ten years as general counsel, I constantly advised employees and our board to think long and hard about what they put in writing, and even longer and harder before pushing the send button on an email. Most employees don't consider the possibility that their documents may be produced in litigation and therefore are often careless in how they write emails and presentations. The difficulty arises when an executive, board member, or employee at any level of an organization makes a statement in writing that on its face may seem benign or is said in jest, or, God forbid, is truly damning. All of those statements are read in hindsight, and hindsight is rarely helpful. Regulators read the documents without the benefit of context. There are no margin notes that say, "Just kidding" or "Hey, this is what I really mean so please don't read this the wrong way." Not surprisingly, the writer's words are interpreted in the worst possible light.

The document production to Justice measured in the millions of pages. We assembled teams of lawyers, most of whom we hired from a company that specializes in document production, to painstakingly review each document. Their job was to determine if it had to be produced to the government and whether it was helpful to our case or, in a worst-case scenario, if it was a smoking gun that could torpedo the merger.

As we dug into the documents, we uncovered areas of concern. The first issue centered on a fare-pricing program that US Airways referred to as "Advantage Pricing." I knew little about this program until Bruce Wark, one of my most trusted advisors and in-house antitrust expert, walked into my office. "Well, we're really going to have to focus on Advantage Pricing," he announced. I had learned over a period of many years that if Bruce told me there was an issue that required close attention, I had better listen carefully. One of the reasons I promoted Bruce to associate general counsel was his knack of taking complex antitrust issues and explaining them in a way that made them sound simple and straightforward.

Bruce told me that Advantage Pricing offered travelers cheap connecting fares as a way for US Airways to compete against its bigger rivals. He then explained how Advantage Pricing worked. The large network carriers, American, United, and Delta, offered nonstop service to a huge number of cities from their mega hubs, while US Airways offered a much smaller number of nonstop flights through its smaller hubs in Phoenix, Charlotte, and Philadelphia.

To remedy this competitive disadvantage, US Airways offered connecting flights to the same destinations as the network carriers, but at a price that was often hundreds of dollars less than the other carriers' nonstop flights. American might charge, say, 1,600 dollars for a nonstop flight between DFW and New York's LaGuardia Airport, while US Airways would charge six hundred dollars for the same itinerary, but with a stop in Philly or Charlotte. The DOJ believed that Advantage Pricing saved consumers tens of millions of dollars and they feared that those cheaper fares would vanish when US Airways combined with American.

Our review also uncovered a series of emails and documents that we wished had never been written. There were several documents penned by US Airways executives suggesting that they would reduce capacity if there were a merger. In DOJ's minds, a reduction in capacity leads to one thing—higher airfares for consumers. These documents gave the DOJ ammunition to argue that the merger would embolden the merged company to slash capacity in an effort to buttress pricing.

While the lawyers worked on the document production and to prepare for upcoming face-to-face meetings with the DOJ, Doug Parker continued his efforts to build the executive team that would lead the new company.

Most of the American executives didn't have a clue whether Parker wanted to keep them around. For me, I had a pretty good idea that he wanted me to stay. Otherwise, what was the point of the breakfast meeting with Scott Kirby a few weeks earlier? I figured that Steve Johnson was out of the picture and had decided to leave the airline once the merger was approved.

Sure enough, Parker scheduled time with me in late February to discuss my future with the company. Like Scott Kirby, Doug asked me to remain as general counsel. I was delighted with the prospect of working for Parker. There was one small hitch that I didn't anticipate. Doug explained that he wanted Steve Johnson to continue in his current role with the company. As such, Parker planned to have the general counsel report directly to Johnson.

The reporting structure suggested by Parker was a problem. As general counsel, I was accustomed to reporting directly to the CEO, with unfiltered access to the board of directors. The idea of having an extra management layer between the CEO and me was not something I thought I could live with. I told Doug that I was anxious to join the new team but needed to report directly to him.

Doug is a good salesman. He praised my work through the bankruptcy and merger and let me know that he had a strong team coming from US Airways and that I would fit in well with them. But, he reiterated that he liked the current arrangement with Steve and didn't plan to change it. He ended the meeting by asking me to think about his offer and to speak with Johnson before making a final decision. I agreed to do that.

Following my meeting with Parker, I called Steve and we set a time to meet. Steve is a savvy guy. He invited me to dinner at the Ritz Carlton in Dallas so we could talk things over in a relaxed atmosphere. Steve is a wine connoisseur and he ordered a bottle of premium red wine. It was a great dinner, but I still wasn't convinced that the new reporting structure would work. It felt like a step backwards to report to anyone other than the CEO and tantamount to a demotion.

Jack Butler soon afterward flew to Dallas to speak with me about the same subject. Despite our differences, Jack and I had developed a mutual respect. We spent nearly two hours behind closed doors in my office. Jack is an eloquent and masterful advocate and he tried hard to persuade me to take the job. He had no vested interest in selecting the executive team so I appreciated the time he sacrificed to meet with me. I was flattered by his efforts, along with those of Parker and Johnson.

In the end, I declined their overtures, knowing it meant the end of my career at American Airlines.

A similar fate awaited most of my colleagues on the American executive team. When Parker completed his selection, only three senior American executives survived the cut—Bev Goulet (chief integration officer), Will Ris (government affairs), and Maya Leibman (information technology). It was not a surprising result. Parker had a long history working with members of his team and he needed to surround himself with people he knew and trusted. Although my tenure at American would soon come to an end, I still had a job to finish. Securing regulatory clearance was at the top of the list.

It was July 2013. It had been five months since we announced the merger with US Airways. Executives from both airlines were growing impatient, desperate to put the regulatory review behind them and finish the deal. I knew we were nowhere near the finish line, but assured Horton and others that formal meetings with Justice would begin soon. We were anxious to resolve the regulatory issues because we had a bankruptcy "confirmation" hearing scheduled for August 15 with Judge Lane. At that hearing, Lane would consider our motion to approve AA's plan of reorganization. Since the centerpiece of that plan hinged on the merger with US Airways, there was no way to get it approved if regulatory issues remained in limbo.

On July 15 and 16, we convened what we believed would be the "last" regularly scheduled meetings of the AMR board of directors, assuming the DOJ did not move to oppose the planned merger. Given the somewhat historic nature of the meetings, we decided to host a dinner at the Perot Museum of Nature and Science in Dallas. We invited our board members, executive officers, and former American Airlines CEOs, along with spouses, to attend the dinner and celebrate the occasion. To top off the list of invitees, we asked Doug Parker and his wife, Gwen, to join the festivities.

It was great to see Bob Crandall, Don Carty, Gerard Arpey, Tom Horton, and Doug Parker in the same room together. Horton and Parker both gave short speeches after dinner, remarking on the notable achievements that resulted in two great airlines joining forces.

After dinner, Crandall pulled me aside and told me he found the whole affair a bit distasteful. "What exactly are we celebrating?" he barked. "The company lost billions of dollars since I left American, labor relations are awful, the company filed for bankruptcy, and you guys managed to give away the company to US Airways. How is that a success?" I understood the point he was making, though it didn't take into consideration the extraordinary events of the previous decade.

A couple weeks later, we finally got the ball rolling with the DOJ. The first big meeting with Justice was scheduled for July 25 in Washington, D.C. "Big" is definitely the operative word. I learned over the years that meetings with Justice are rarely intimate affairs with just a handful of people. Instead, they are large gatherings. American and US Airways each brought seven or eight people to the meeting, including our outside lawyers and economists. Justice, on the other hand, invited a gaggle of people to the meeting. I counted a total of thirty-eight to forty people in attendance on their side of the table. I am sure that number included a handful of "summers" (law school interns), but it didn't really matter who they were. It was overkill and a waste of taxpayer money.

The meeting dragged on for nearly four hours. During that time, Justice Department lawyers and economists laid out a series of concerns—that we would discontinue Advantage Pricing, that the combined airline would reduce capacity, that airfares would increase, and that the concentration of slot holdings at capacity-constrained airports, like Washington Reagan and New York LaGuardia, were too large. The list of objections was long.

As I listened to Department of Justice officials outline their concerns, I recall thinking with growing alarm that these guys really believe what they are saying. This isn't just a negotiating ploy. They really don't like this deal. Some of the attorneys in the room had been battling with American for well over twenty-five years and I wondered if this was their swan song. Perhaps it was their way of getting even for previous fights with American, ones that stuck with them all these years later.

American's relationship with the DOJ vacillated somewhere between cautious and strained. One of American's early fights with Justice centered on a well-known episode involving Bob Crandall that occurred in 1982. In those days, American and Braniff Airways both had substantial operations at DFW Airport and were vicious competitors. Both airlines were suffering enormous losses as a result of fare wars between the two airlines. Crandall, then president of American, telephoned Braniff's CEO, Howard Putnam. Putnam returned the call. During their conversation, Crandall groused about the destructive competition between the two carriers at DFW.

"Do you have a suggestion for me?" Putnam asked.

"Yes, I have a suggestion for you," Crandall replied. "Raise your goddamn fares 20 percent. I'll raise mine the next morning....You'll make more money and I will, too."

"We can"t talk about pricing," Putnam protested.

"Oh [expletive], Howard, we can talk about any goddamn thing we want to talk about," Crandall said.

Unfortunately for Crandall, Putnam recorded the call and turned over the transcript to the Justice Department.

The Justice Department sued American and Crandall in February 1983 in Federal District Court in Dallas, claiming that the company and Crandall violated U.S. antitrust laws. The lawsuit was later settled, with Crandall agreeing to strict record keeping requirements of phone calls with other airline executives. There was no admission by American or Crandall of any wrongdoing.

On another occasion, in 1999, the Justice Department filed a lawsuit against American in Wichita, Kansas, claiming that the company had engaged in "predatory pricing" in a fight with three small air carriers, Vanguard Airlines, Sun Jet International Airlines and Western Pacific Airlines. But, in 2001, U.S. District Judge J. Thomas Marten dismissed the case and threw Justice out on its ear. "There is no doubt that American may be a difficult, vigorous, even brutal competitor," Marten said in his decision, "but here, it engaged only in bare, not brass, knuckle competition." The 10th Circuit Court of Appeals affirmed the decision in 2003 after DOJ attorneys appealed the Wichita verdict.

I can't say for sure that the attorneys from Justice were itching for a rematch, but many of the same attorneys who worked on the Wichita case were still hanging around in 2013. We had several other skirmishes with Justice over the years and I always had the sense that those attorneys carried a grudge against American and were anxious for another fight.

Cognizant of the history with Justice, the AA and US Airways teams countered each of DOJ's concerns, but did so in a deferential manner, trying hard to keep the conversation civil, knowing we had a long road in front of us. The more I listened, the more I got the sense they were not buying what we were selling. I recalled MJ Moltenbrey's reference to the merger caboose. Privately, I wondered if it was possible that the deal could be in genuine peril? Would DOJ actually consider enjoining the transaction?

After listening to the department's lawyers for so many hours, Steve Johnson had had enough. Near the close of the meeting he stood up, looked around the room, and told the DOJ that their position regarding capacity reductions was "totally ludicrous." Steve had the temerity to say what we'd all been thinking and I admired his conviction of principle. I'm not sure I agreed with his timing and choice of delivery, but his message was delivered loud and clear.

Additional meetings with Justice were scheduled for early August, with a final meeting set for Tuesday, August 6. We worked the entire weekend to prepare for the meeting. We added, subtracted, discarded, and modified the presentation; we debated who was going to speak, what they would say, and in which order the spokespersons would make their remarks. Achieving consensus among a large group of egocentric lawyers and economists was a mind-numbing affair.

On the day of the final meeting, we piled into several taxis and met outside the entrance to the DOJ office building. Gaining security clearance to enter high-profile federal offices in Washington, D.C., is a time-consuming affair so we arrived a full 30 minutes before our meeting was set to begin. Once everyone cleared security, we were escorted upstairs to the meeting room.

Everyone in attendance knew this meeting was the final showdown. For us, it represented our last opportunity to persuade the government that the consumer benefits attendant to a combination of American Airlines and US Airways far surpassed any perceived harm to the consumer. What we did not know, and never will know with any certainty, is whether the government had already made up its mind before we ever walked into the room.

Bill Baer, who was then serving as assistant U.S. attorney, headed up the meeting on behalf of the Justice Department. At his side, Renata Hesse, then deputy assistant attorney general, was second in command and in charge of the day-to-day handling of the investigation. Before accepting his position at Justice, Baer worked as a partner at Arnold & Porter, an exclusive, high-powered Washington, D.C., law firm and served for many years at the Federal Trade Commission. While Baer gained extensive antitrust experience working at the law firm and at the FTC, he had little experience inside the Justice Department. The U.S. Senate had confirmed his appointment just nine months earlier in December 2012, and he was sworn into office on January 3, just six weeks before we announced our merger.

On the other end of the spectrum, Renata Hesse was a longtime attorney in the department and brought plenty of experience to the table. Hesse has worked at Justice for more than fifteen years, along with a stint as senior counsel at the Federal Communications Commission, where she oversaw AT&T's failed bid to acquire T-Mobile.

Once all parties were seated, Baer opened the meeting and allowed us to begin our presentation. We didn't get very far before he started to pepper the AA/US team with questions. He is a colorful personality and made no effort to mask his misgivings about the proposed merger. I got the distinct impression that he relished the banter. Baer's reservations went much deeper than the issues directly at hand. He and the staff seemed intent on using this deal as a proxy to resolve a number of perceived competitive issues in the airline industry.

To counter Baer's arguments, we used every resource in our arsenal. We repackaged old arguments into new ones, we highlighted the enormous consumer benefits that would flow from the merger, and we trotted out a "list of horribles" that would ensue if Justice opposed the merger. American's outside counsel, Joe Sims, and US Airways' counsel, Paul Denis (a senior antitrust partner at the prestigious Dechert law firm) went toe to toe with Baer and did a great job responding to Baer's concerns. I was confident they had advanced the ball with Justice.

Because the merger was at the heart of American's planned emergence from bankruptcy, the department wanted to know what would happen to American and its employees and creditors if Justice moved to block the merger. As the senior American Airlines representative at the meeting, I made a determined plea on behalf of our constituents. In doing so, I warned Baer that the consequences of a failed merger would be widespread and an enormous blow to the company.

I told Baer that American would be forced to retreat to its independent plan, one that did not yet have the backing of creditors or employees. I reminded him that unlike most merger scenarios, our unionized workforce was in full support of the merger and that a failed merger would wreak havoc on American's relationship with labor. I also told him that creditor claims would be placed in jeopardy and that equity holders would suffer greatly.

The creditors' committee wanted me to suggest that all would be lost if the merger failed and that American had no viable alternative. I refused to paint a picture that bleak because it was not accurate. The meeting concluded, with no indication from Justice as to how they might proceed. We remained in the dark.

We walked out of the building and met on the sidewalk just outside DOJ's offices. It was midafternoon, with the sun blazing overhead, a hot and humid day in the nation's capital. A dozen or so of us, all in work attire—suits, ties, jackets—stood in a makeshift huddle in the sweltering heat. Retreating to a spacious air-conditioned office would have been a more prudent locale for an impromptu meeting, but everyone was anxious to exchange views, hoping to convince one another about what it all meant and what DOJ would do.

At this point, listening *ad nauseam* to a postmortem was of little value. The only thing that interested me now was the bottom line. Did counsel believe that DOJ would sue to block the transaction? Nothing else really mattered at that moment. Joe Sims was one of the first to speak: "Baer has serious concerns about this merger but at the end of the day, I do not believe Justice will sue. They will demand big concessions, but I can't see them trying to stop the deal. There is simply too much at stake." MJ did not agree. "They will sue us to block the transaction."

It was simply too hot to continue the ad hoc sidewalk confab. Once I heard counsels' views, I was ready to call it a day, head to the airport, and return to Dallas. It was now a waiting game. The DOJ promised to give us their answer by August 9, just three days later. There was nothing more we could do.

August 9 came and went. No word from Baer. Sims called him and pressed Baer for a definitive deadline, reminding him of the August 15 hearing in bankruptcy court. Baer didn't budge, merely telling Sims they needed more time.

On the morning of August 13, I arrived at work and parked in my usual spot in the garage. I entered the lobby of the headquarters building and headed to the stairway adjacent to the elevators for my customary walk up the five flights of stairs.

When I reached the third floor, I heard the familiar notification on my cell phone indicating an incoming email message. I reached for my phone as I continued to walk and read the four-word message.

"Holy shit" I blurted out.

I looked up and noticed the startled look on a woman's face as she passed me on her way down the stairs. I issued a quick apology and continued up the last flights of stairs, but now at an accelerated pace.

CHAPTER 18

SEARCHING FOR A WAY FORWARD

I walked straight to Tom Horton's office, not stopping at my desk to drop off my briefcase. After so many years as general counsel, I was accustomed to delivering bad news, but this felt different. This time it was squarely on my shoulders and I couldn't shake the feeling of dread and disappointment.

As I entered Horton's office, I attempted to convey a calm, measured tone despite the gravity of the message I was about to share. I read aloud the email I received from Joe Sims: "They are filing today." Tom's mouth dropped open and he stared at me in disbelief. Neither of us said much, knowing it was going to be a rough day with lots of moving pieces. Horton asked his assistant to see if she could get Armando Codina, our lead director, on the phone. As she patched him through, we gave Codina the bad news. It was a short conversation. We agreed to assemble the full board on a 9:30 a.m. conference call.

I had little more than an hour before the board call. I was in scramble mode. My biggest challenge at that moment: The lawsuit hadn't yet been filed so I couldn't read the complaint before the call. But I knew there were several questions that had to be answered.

How long will it take to get to trial? Can we hold the company together while we fight with the government? Do we have the best litigation team in place? Will we win?

There was one other topic that I expected one of the board members to raise: "How the hell did this happen?" I had assured the board that we would easily achieve regulatory approval and I was dead wrong. It was a legitimate line of inquiry. I didn't want to sound defensive, but I had been careful to walk back my assurances over the last two months and warned the board that a lawsuit was a distinct possibility.

The board had grown accustomed to last-minute requests to participate in crisis-laden discussions, so this request was not unusual. The short notice was emblematic of American's operating environment during the last ten years. Our board members had a vast array of commitments, including board positions on some of the largest public companies in the country, but without hesitation, they dropped what they were doing that morning and dialed into the call.

They were attentive as we explained the state of play. One issue, arguably the principal challenge we faced, was at the heart of the discussion—how long could we keep the merger alive now that the full weight of the U.S. government was dedicated to stopping the merger in its tracks? I did not have a good answer to the question. Neither did our outside counsel.

The recent history of merger transactions opposed by the government was not encouraging. Fresh on our minds was the aborted 39 billion-dollar AT&T merger with T-Mobile. The parties announced that deal in March 2011 and immediately came under fire from federal regulators (including Renata Hesse, who was in charge of our investigation). After prolonged opposition from the government, the parties pulled the plug and abandoned the deal nine months later.

I also recalled United Airlines' attempt to buy US Airways in May 2000. The DOJ's review dragged on for over a year before finally announcing its intention to block the merger as anticompetitive. The government's announcement, in July 2001, was all it took to convince United and US Airways to cancel their planned union. They did so by the end of that same day.

We found ourselves faced with the same dilemma. We believed in the merits of the merger and had too much at stake to simply give up. Backing out would throw the company into chaos and create untold numbers of difficulties. At that moment, it was too distasteful to even contemplate labor's reaction if we threw in the towel without a fight. I tried not to get ahead of myself. I hadn't yet seen a copy of the complaint. The legal team needed time to evaluate the merits of the DOJ's arguments so we could intelligently assess the size of the mountain that lay ahead.

Bill Baer, U.S. assistant attorney general, held a telephonic Q&A news conference on the morning he filed the lawsuit. His answers to reporters' questions were filled with chest-pounding rhetoric, as if the merger was the devil incarnate, set to gouge the wallet of the traveling public and trample the competition. It was a little hard to swallow.

When asked why the department filed to enjoin the merger after it had approved three mergers involving American's largest competitors, Baer remarked that while shareholders and creditors might benefit from consolidation, "The fact of the matter is that consumers will get the shaft." He went on to say, "This merger is premised not on increase[d] competition between the legacy carriers, but on the notion that it will allow the new American to compete less."

Describing US Airways, he claimed, "They don't want to compete. They basically want to fly where they want to fly without competition." Baer characterized the proposed deal as "pretty messed up" and one that is "pretty bad for consumers."

On its face, the allegations in the fifty-six-page lawsuit told an interesting story. The complaint focused on recent consolidation in the industry, the decline in competition among large airlines, and the resulting harm to consumers. The complaint suggested that a merger of American and US Airways would "make it easier for the remaining airlines to cooperate, rather than compete on price and service." It alleged that consolidation led to "capacity discipline," a reference to efforts to restrain growth or reduce established air service as a means to boost airfares.

The complaint was replete with words drawn directly from the mouths of AA and US Airways executives. It cited a US Airways executive who referred to consolidation in the industry as the "New Holy Grail" and an AA analysis that concluded, "Following a merger, carriers tend to remove capacity or grow more slowly than the rest of the industry." A US Airways document added further flame to the consolidation fire when Parker stated in 2010 that the industry had yet to hit its "sweet spot" and that additional consolidation was needed because the industry remained "overly fragmented."

The government's lawsuit directed its angst at other capacity-related statements made by US Airways and American. Paragraph 67 of the lawsuit stated, in part:

> US Airways believes that merging with American "finishes industry evolution" by accomplishing US Airways' goal of "reduc[ing] capacity more efficiently." When first considering a combination with American, US Airways projected that the merged firm could reduce capacity by as much as 10 percent. Similarly, American expects that the merger will lead to capacity reductions that would negatively impact "communities," "people," "customers," and "suppliers." Higher fares would be just around the corner.

Another issue that chapped DOJ's hide was the resulting concentration of gates and slots at Ronald Reagan Washington National Airport. Reagan Washington, or DCA (its three-letter airport code), is one of only a few airports in the country that has FAA "takeoff and landing slots" (although the FAA recently announced the easing of slot restrictions at the Newark airport). As a result of an earlier deal with Delta, US Airways controlled 55 percent of the slots at DCA, with American holding 14 percent. After the merger, the new company would control 69 percent of all slots, and DOJ found that level of slot concentration unacceptable.

"Without slots, other airlines cannot enter or expand the number of flights that they offer on other routes," it argued. "As a result, Washington, D.C.-area passengers would likely see higher fares and fewer choices if the merger were approved."

US Airways' Advantage Fares, an issue we debated with Baer and Hesse on multiple occasions, got top billing in the complaint. Baer and company believed that the newly combined company would eliminate Advantage Fares once the merger closed. The DOJ argued that "if the merger were approved, US Airways' economic rationale for offering Advantage Fares would likely go away...The bottom line is that the merged airline would likely abandon Advantage Fares, eliminating significant competition and causing consumers to pay hundreds of millions of dollars more."

After reviewing the complaint, Bruce Wark and I got on the phone with our antitrust lawyers. There was one universal sentiment that came out of the call—the allegations in the complaint were written in a way that left little room for a settlement. Often, companies agree to disgorge assets as a means of relieving anticompetitive effects of a merger so they can resolve open issues with the DOJ and close the merger. In this case, disgorging assets (like slots and gates at DCA) would address one narrow issue in the complaint. It would not address global industry-wide issues, things like capacity discipline, Advantage Fares, and airline cooperation.

Even Bill Baer conceded that there was little prospect for settlement. "If anybody wants to come to us to propose a settlement, we're always prepared to listen," he said on the August 13 telephone conference with reporters. "But our view, looking at the evidence before us, is that the right outcome here is a full-stop injunction."

The United States government was not the only enemy on the battlefield. Six states—Arizona, Virginia, Florida, Pennsylvania, Tennessee, and, oddly enough, Texas—plus the District of Columbia, led by their respective state attorneys general, sided with the government and joined the lawsuit as plaintiffs. (A seventh state, Michigan, joined as a plaintiff in early September.) It was easy to understand why states like Arizona, Pennsylvania, Virginia, and the District of Columbia decided to join the fray. Arizona stood to lose US Airways as a corporate headquarters and faced a possible downsizing of the Phoenix hub. The same rationale applied to Pennsylvania as it considered the future of its Philadelphia hub. The District of Columbia and Virginia, perhaps influenced by U.S. senators and representatives, coveted slots at DCA, and the future utilization of those slots may have played a role in their decision to oppose the merger.

But there was one plaintiff that defied rational explanation. That distinction was reserved for the State of Texas. When I read the complaint and saw that Texas, led by its attorney general and future governor, Greg Abbott, had joined the lawsuit, I was speechless. It made no sense. Abbott is a staunch Republican and was a vocal critic of then President Barack Obama. In 2013, when asked about his job as attorney general, Abbott reportedly said, "I go into the office in the morning, I sue Barack Obama, and then I go home."

It was impossible to figure out how Attorney General Abbott reconciled his disdain for the Obama administration with his willingness to join forces with the administration to derail a planned business combination that would shower untold benefits on his home state. Texas would be the corporate home of the combined company, with the potential for significant increases in employment and collateral benefits.

Even more shocking was the fact that when United and Continental merged in 2010, Abbott did not contest that merger even though the headquarters of the new airline would be located in Chicago, not Houston, Continental's then home base. I was left to ponder two questions: How in the world did Abbott's advisors convince him to join hands with Justice, and what were we going to do about it?

Immediately following the board call, we circulated a joint media statement with US Airways, decrying the actions of the federal government and assuring employees and financial constituents that we would fight the lawsuit to conclusion:

We believe that the DOJ is wrong in its assessment of our merger. Integrating the complementary networks of American and US Airways to benefit passengers is the motivation for bringing these airlines together...We will mount a vigorous defense and pursue all legal remedies in order to achieve this merger and deliver the benefits of the new American to our customers and communities as soon as possible.

Public statements were one thing; the prospect of beating the government in a lawsuit was quite another. By late afternoon, reality began to sink in. The lawsuit that Baer unleashed and dumped at our feet would be a difficult fight to win. At that moment, I had no idea if we could prevail at trial. While I disagreed with the DOJ's conclusions, Baer did a nice job setting forth the rationale behind his decision to oppose the merger.

My new friends at US Airways had no such doubts. They made it clear from the outset that we would win, no questions asked. Their confidence, bordering on hubris, was not surprising. It was consistent with the demeanor they displayed during merger negotiations. Though I tried to embrace their enthusiasm, I was worried. It was impossible to be certain how the trial would unfold.

I knew my day wouldn't be complete without hearing from Jack Butler. Sure enough, my phone rang later that afternoon and I instantly recognized the number as belonging to Butler. He got right to the point. Jack indicated that he and the UCC were concerned that American would use the lawsuit as a pretext to walk away from the merger. Butler sounded accusatory. He was suspicious and it seemed that he thought everything American did was laced with nefarious motives.

I explained to Jack that we planned to vigorously oppose the government's lawsuit, but had a fiduciary duty to begin work on a backup plan. We couldn't just hope and pray that we beat the government. What would happen, I argued, if we lost and did nothing in advance to prepare for that potential outcome?

Butler found my explanation weak and unacceptable. He claimed that contingency planning would detract from our efforts to fight the lawsuit. He vowed to oppose any effort to devote resources on a contingency plan. I'm afraid my exhortation did nothing but fan the flames of mistrust. He warned that if we lost at trial, the UCC would demand significant modifications to the independent plan, including management changes at the top of the organization. I knew

Tom Horton was on Butler's list, along with a few other executives, including our senior vice president of marketing, Virasb Vahidi, but I let it go. Management of the airline was way outside the UCC's purview, but I saw no reason to fight with Butler at that point.

Horton and I were way ahead of Jack Butler. We had already engaged in multiple conversations about contingency planning long before the DOJ decided to sue. To his credit, Tom believed we should work full speed on two parallel tracks—fight the lawsuit, yet convince the UCC and other constituencies to work with us to polish the independent plan. It was a laudable goal, but we both knew it would be an uphill battle to convince anyone to devote energy to a Plan B with the lawsuit pending.

It was early evening on the day the government filed its lawsuit. I was in my office and had just completed a case strategy conference call with our outside lawyers when one of the senior officers stuck his head in the door. Apparently, I was needed in Jim Ream's office for an important meeting. I thought it was an odd place for a meeting. Ream was the senior vice president of maintenance and didn't have direct involvement in the bankruptcy or the DOJ lawsuit. As I approached his office, I noticed the door was closed. We rarely discussed matters behind closed doors so I figured something was out of whack.

When I walked in, there were seven senior officers seated around Ream's conference table. What surprised me most was the three bottles of wine on the table. Alcohol on the premises was strictly forbidden and a violation of our rules of conduct. The exception to the "Boy Scout" style of senior management was Jim Ream, so I wasn't surprised that he was the instigator of the spontaneous happy hour. "What's going on?" I asked.

Ream was not the kind of guy who paid close attention to corporate rules. He was laser-focused on maintenance and safety. As long as our aircraft were properly maintained and getting off the gate without mechanical problems, Ream figured the rest of the rules didn't apply to him. A couple years earlier I received a complaint from a maintenance employee that Jim had a habit of using excessive amounts of profanity on morning conference calls. I met with

Ream and asked him to tone it down. He gave me one of those "are you kidding me" kind of looks and walked out of my office.

Ream explained the purpose for his gathering. "After all the shit that happened today, I figured we all needed a drink and I was more than happy to make that happen. Besides, we need you here to tell us whether this shit from the government is going to stick."

As general counsel, I was supposed to enforce the rules, but on this occasion, I didn't care. What were they going to do—fire me? I gladly accepted a glass of red wine and joined the group. All eyes were on me, and everyone wanted to know what happened and whether we were going to win. My answers were no better then than they were earlier in the day—I didn't know what happened and I didn't know if we could win.

Dan Garton, our CEO of American Eagle and former executive vice president of marketing, made a competition out of almost everything, so he came up with an idea to add some fun to our impromptu meeting. "Let's take a straw vote. Write down 'win' or 'lose' on a piece of paper and let's see how it turns out." He quickly handed out a piece of scrap paper to everyone. We all wrote our prediction, folded our papers and gave them to Garton to tally the votes.

"It's a tie," he announced with a hearty laugh. "Four votes that we win the lawsuit and four that we lose." "That's exactly the problem," I said. "The whole thing is a crapshoot. We've got to find a way to settle this damn thing."

Two days later, August 15, I arrived at the bankruptcy court for our confirmation hearing. Judge Lane was in a testy mood. Now that the government's lawsuit had thrown our bankruptcy plan into no-man's-land, he was peeved that we intended to go forward with the hearing. A misbehaving air conditioner in the courtroom on a hot day in New York City contributed to his poor frame of mind. He wanted us to adjourn the hearing until the government's case was resolved.

Steve Karotkin and Jack Butler, through some adept lawyering, managed to convince Lane to let us go forward with the hearing, but he was still unhappy about it. "I have lingering doubts whether this approach is the most efficient or prudent under the circumstances, particularly given that the court has numerous other matters and cases to address and is operating on budget restrictions imposed by sequestration," Lane said, referring to the pending government shutdown caused by a legislative impasse. "But, I think it's the best we can do under these circumstances."

At the conclusion of the hearing, Lane did not rule from the bench but it was good to get the hearing behind us. Now all we needed to do was find a way to beat the government so we could complete the confirmation process and close the merger.

On August 23, I was on an early morning flight to Washington for meetings with trial counsel. I made a habit of connecting to inflight Wi-Fi as soon as we took off. Midway through the flight, I received an urgent email message from Andy Backover, American's vice president of corporate communications, requesting that I call him as soon as I landed. I asked why. He told me Horton was fuming about an article published that morning in *The Dallas Morning News*.

I didn't have to ask Andy further questions. I had a pretty good idea why Horton was upset. Several days earlier, Mark Curriden, the owner and publisher of *The Texas Lawbook*, the state's largest online legal periodical, interviewed me shortly after the DOJ filed its lawsuit. Curriden ran an extensive story in the *Lawbook* about the litigation and American's plans going forward. The article was picked up by *The Dallas Morning News* and that's what caused all the ruckus.

During the interview, Curriden asked me point-blank whether we had a backup plan if the government prevailed at trial. I told Curriden, "No, we do not have a Plan B."

Publicly acknowledging that the company did not have an alternative plan sounded like nails on a chalkboard to Horton and our public relations team. Just as Butler, et al. were opposed to us even talking about an alternative plan, Horton and the PR folks were adamant that it was essential to convey American's strength and future viability regardless of the government's effort to enjoin the merger. That meant developing a Plan B. I shared their view, but thought it equally important to convey that the company was fully committed to the merger, and that we were not using the government's lawsuit as a pretext to achieve a different outcome. It was uncomfortable to be at odds with my boss, and I recall wishing that I'd chosen different words during the interview.

I found myself getting punched from two directions: by Jack Butler's opposition to a Plan B, and Tom Horton's anger that I said we had no Plan B. It was one of those days.

As time passed, the rift between American and the UCC advisors grew ever larger. They convinced themselves that we were up to no good, secretly plotting to promote our independent plan while paying lip service to the litigation. It reminded me of the sentiment that permeated the merger negotiations a year earlier. At that time, the UCC didn't trust that American would negotiate in good faith with US Airways; this time around they didn't trust that we wanted to fight the government's lawsuit.

Every move we made was analyzed under the microscope of alleged bad intentions. In the minds of the UCC advisors, there were ghosts in every corner. At one point, false allegations surfaced that Horton had dinner with various labor leaders in an effort to convince them to support the independent plan. On another occasion, the UCC complained that we replaced a pro merger video banner on the monitors at our gates with advertising for a new animated children's movie entitled "Planes," a movie that featured American Airlines aircraft.

Both US Airways and American engaged top-notch litigators to defeat the DOJ. US Airways hired Rich Parker, a senior litigation partner at O'Melveny & Myers. O'Melveny is a well-known, seven hundred-lawyer firm based in Los Angeles. Rich Parker is a straight-talking, no-nonsense lawyer, with a cowboy drawl and an irreverent sense of humor. Parker is a graduate of the UCLA law school and a well-known antitrust specialist. I have no idea where he picked up his style of speech, but it is both disarming and folksy.

For American, we already had Joe Sims and Bruce McDonald, a former deputy assistant attorney general at DOJ, from Jones Day on the payroll, and we added one of their top antitrust litigators, John Majoras, to the team.

The most critical issue we faced at the outset of the litigation came down to one thing—the date of the trial. We needed the trial to start as quickly as possible. The reason was obvious. The DOJ's lawsuit created tremendous uncertainty for all constituencies, and we needed a speedy resolution or the merger would collapse under its own weight. Naturally, the DOJ knew of our dilemma and they wanted a trial date as far out in the future as possible. A lengthy delay would kill the deal.

The judge assigned to hear the case would set the trial date. That responsibility fell to Federal District Judge Colleen Kollar-Kotelly, a 1997 Clinton appointee. Judge Kollar-Kotelly was no stranger to the DOJ, having worked in the Criminal Division for three years early in her legal career. She assumed responsibility for the Microsoft antitrust case after the previous judge was removed from the proceeding. I was buoyed by the knowledge that our fate was in the hands of an experienced jurist.

We filed a motion with Kollar-Kotelly requesting a trial date of November 12, 2013, just 11 weeks hence. It was an aggressive position. It would be a major undertaking for both sides to be ready in such a short period of time. In most complex civil litigation cases, trial dates are set a year or more after a lawsuit is filed. The preparation for a trial with the DOJ, which has enormous resources, is immense. Eleven weeks meant that lawyers from all sides would work every day and every night. Sleep would have the value of a rare gem.

The DOJ countered with a trial date no earlier than March 3, 2014. If the judge accepted the government's proposal, we were sunk. It would be difficult, if not impossible, to keep the merger alive for seven months while we awaited trial.

Both sides prepared briefs in support of their respective positions and the judge made her ruling on August 30. We were elated when she announced that the trial would begin November 25, the Monday before Thanksgiving. It was a huge victory. With an early trial date, we now had a fighting chance to keep the merger alive.

With the trial date set, all eyes and all hands turned to trial preparation. The sheer size of the trial team felt at times larger than the population of a small country. A steady stream of lawyers and paralegals scurried to and fro. Some worked on document production, already measuring in the millions of pages of documents. Others worked on witness deposition prep (with certain witnesses requiring a lot of attention to ready them for a multi-hour grilling at the hands of a DOJ lawyer). Still other attorneys met with expert witnesses, principally economists whose task it would be to make sense of mind- numbing econometric models like the Herfindahl-Hirschman Index used to measure market concentration.

As the legal team prepared for trial, employee groups explored ways to apply pressure on the DOJ in an attempt to influence the outcome. The DOJ is, by design, structured as an apolitical body and allegedly not subject to political whim or public sentiment. That may be the design, but the reality is much different. It is difficult, if not impossible, for a high-profile government agency to be completely insulated from its fellow citizens and current events.

The public relations departments of both companies operated in overdrive. The PR departments inundated the legal teams with hundreds of updates, conference calls, position papers, media issues, and never-ending streams of questions. Leaving no stone unturned, they filled the airwaves, media outlets, and employee communication portals with mounds of information hyping the benefits of the proposed merger. The PR campaign, while well-intentioned and successful, required constant legal intervention and supervision. The PR tail was definitely wagging the head of the legal dog. I quickly reached a saturation point. During one of many all-hands conference calls, I pleaded with the PR folks to back off and let us do our job. While a series of affirmative responses portrayed agreement with my request, nothing changed. We hovered in the airspace of public relations bedlam for the duration of the litigation.

On the political front, both airlines engaged in extensive congressional lobbying. The effort was designed to build support for the merger and blunt public criticism offered by some members of Congress. The American Airlines officer in charge of all things political was Will Ris, American's senior vice president of government affairs.

Ris possessed an uncanny ability to talk people into doing things they don't want to do. Over the years, he roped me into several work projects that were painful and uncomfortable. Will played to a person's sense of company duty and loyalty, sprinkled with a large dose of flattery, whenever he needed help with a particularly sensitive subject.

A few days after the merger was announced on February 14, 2013, Will called me and asked how things were progressing. He told me I was a terrific general counsel and that the company was fortunate to have me leading the charge. I knew I was being set up. Will eventually weaved his way to the subject at hand. He told me that the House of Representatives planned to hold hearings on the merger and said I would be the perfect witness to testify for American. I unleashed a series of objections, but to no avail. Once Will baits the line and sets the hook, he doesn't let go until the fish is flapping on shore. After several minutes listening to Will's exhortations, including hollow promises that my testimony and questioning from Congress would be a simple task, I relented.

Steve Johnson received a similar rope-a-dope treatment and agreed to testify as US Airways' representative at the congressional hearing. The hearing was set for February 26 before the House Judiciary Committee. As the hearing date drew near, we finalized our written testimony and submitted it to the committee. Preparation for questioning by members of Congress was long and arduous, including a full day of mock questioning by a panel of outside consultants and advisors. The group stressed one point time and again. They admonished us not to say anything during the hearing that would damage our case with the DOJ. In other words, they warned against saying anything stupid. They didn't care if we hit a home run, they just didn't want a strikeout.

The day of the hearing arrived. As I took my seat at the witness table, I looked behind me and desperately wanted to trade places with someone seated in the spectator seats. The name Will Ris came to mind. The hearing came to order and I read my testimony into the record. As the committee members started firing questions at the witnesses (the part of the proceeding I dreaded most), I found myself enjoying the experience immensely. I realized that after twenty-nine years in the airline business, I doubted that a lay congressional representative could ask a question that I was ill prepared to answer. I actually relished the opportunity to educate members of Congress regarding the tremendous merger benefits that would flow to their constituents, and how the merger would strengthen the nation's air transportation system. Overall, the hearing went well and neither Steve nor I said anything that came even close to a strikeout.

Three months later, Will invited my wife and me to attend a concert at the White House. I suspect it was Will's way of saying thank you for twisting my arm to testify at the congressional hearing. The concert was worth the pain of a congressional hearing. What a cool event it was—the Library of Congress Gershwin Award, honoring Carole King. The evening included a photo op with President Obama and the First Lady. While we waited for our 30 seconds with the President, we "mingled" in the State Dining Room with the likes of Billy Joel, Gloria Estefan, and James Taylor. Hanging on one of the walls of the dining room is a famous portrait of Abraham Lincoln. As I stared at the painting, a woman next to me commented, "Wow, that's a beautiful portrait of Daniel Day Lewis. He sure looks a lot like Abraham Lincoln." I glanced in the woman's direction, ready to explain that in fact it was Lincoln's portrait, when she smiled knowingly as if to say "almost gotcha." It was country music superstar Trisha Yearwood. "Yes, it's an uncanny likeness," I agreed.

A few weeks later, Will Ris called again and asked me to testify a second time, on this occasion in front of the Senate Commerce, Science and Transportation Committee. I gladly accepted. After the White House adventure, how could I refuse? This time I would sit on the panel with Doug Parker. Will assured me that the senators would not have much interest in questioning a lame duck general counsel, when they could instead direct their questions to the CEO designate of the new American Airlines. Will's assessment proved accurate. Other than reading my testimony into the record, I hardly got a chance to speak before the hearing adjourned.

With trial preparation, a PR campaign, and a lobbying effort barreling down the runway at full speed, my thoughts turned to settlement. Was there a way we could broker a deal with Justice and avoid the risk attendant to a trial? Our fate was in the hands of Judge Kollar-Kotelly, and no matter her years of experience and praise as a fair-minded jurist, I desperately wanted to find a way to settle the case.

From the outset, there was little equivocation on the part of US Airways about our chances at trial. They remained steadfast in their belief that we would prevail, no questions asked. Steve Johnson once remarked, in a team conference call, that we were "kicking the DOJ's ass." His assessment may have been accurate, but I had a difficult time mustering the same level of confidence.

I recall a conversation with Steve in August to discuss how best to communicate with our teams as we prepared for trial. He likened the role of a general counsel in times of hardship to a "cheerleader," saying that it was our job to keep the team focused on the task at hand, to remain positive and optimistic. I certainly didn't disagree with his assessment, but told him that I questioned whether we could prevail at trial. I remarked that we had already failed once when we assured our boards that the DOJ would not seek to enjoin the merger, and that a loss at trial would have profound consequences for both companies. On this last point, we agreed—there was much at stake and we needed to win.

Steve and I both pondered what it meant to "win." We believed that a reasonable settlement, one that did not materially diminish the value of the merger synergies, would easily qualify as a win. The big question, given the issues raised by the DOJ, was how to get there. As it turned out, the first step toward settlement began, not with the DOJ, but with the attorney general of the State of Texas.

CHAPTER 19

LET'S MAKE A DEAL

O n one of the few days in August that I was not in Washington, D.C., I completed a series of meetings in my conference room and walked to the desk of my assistant, Heather. She handed me a phone message. It was from Wayne Watts, who was general counsel at AT&T. I had no idea what he wanted, but dialed his number.

"Wayne, this is Gary Kennedy returning your call. How are you?"

"Doing well. How are you holding up?" Watts asked.

"It's a battle. You know that better than anyone." I imagined that Watts still felt the sting of the DOJ's August 2011 lawsuit to block his company's efforts to buy T-Mobile. "I would be doing a hell of a lot better if I could get this merger closed," I told Watts.

"That's why I'm calling with a piece of advice. I don't know what happened between your company and Abbott, but I think you've got a real opportunity to get Texas out of the lawsuit. You need to call Abbott's chief of staff, Daniel Hodge, and set a time to meet with him. I think you can get a deal."

"I'm definitely interested in a deal. I'll call Hodge today." I thanked Watts for his advice and hung up the phone.

I dialed Bruce Wark's number and asked him to stop by my office. I relayed the substance of my conversation with Watts, and together we placed a call to Hodge. I think Hodge may have been expecting our call. He agreed to meet as soon as we could get ourselves to Austin.

Bruce and I flew to Austin a few days later. It didn't take long to realize that Attorney General Abbott's staff wanted out of the lawsuit and they wanted to do it quickly. Abbott must have experienced buyer's remorse soon after the State of Texas signed on as a plaintiff. Abbott was in the middle of a campaign for Texas governor against Texas State Senator Wendy Davis, and the lawsuit was like a neon-lit theater marquee advertising a coming attraction: "Worst Decision by a Politician, Starring Attorney General Greg Abbott."

While discussions were underway with the State of Texas, we decided to make a similar overture to the DOJ, despite the fact that the lawsuit, as written, provided little prospect of settlement. The idea was to offer "behavioral" remedies to the government, designed to address a number of problems identified in the lawsuit. Behavioral remedies deal with airline conduct, things like capacity reductions and the downsizing or closing of hub airports. After the settlement proposal was presented to Bill Baer, it didn't take long to get a response.

"He called it a fuck knuckle." Joe Sims was referring to Baer's characterization of our settlement proposal.

I wasn't sure I heard Joe correctly. "What did he call it?"

"You heard me. He called our settlement proposal a fuck knuckle."

I was standing in Sims' D.C. office. I looked at him and said, "What the hell is a fuck knuckle?"

"I have no idea, but it can't be good."

Joe was right. The DOJ said our proposed behavioral remedies were nonstarters. They had no interest in these kinds of remedies. But, there was a glimmer of good news. Even though Baer dismissed our proposal out of hand, he made a comment that was encouraging. He told Sims and Rich Parker that the DOJ was open to considering a package of structural remedies, meaning a divestiture of assets.

I was ecstatic. You never know what your adversary in a commercial dispute is really thinking, how they are evaluating their case, what weaknesses they perceive, whether they are anxious for a way out. Here, the only thing we knew for certain is that the DOJ had opened the door a crack. Why did they do this? No one knew. Whatever the reason, I was anxious to push the door open as far as it would go. Others on the team were less optimistic. They did not believe Baer's overture would amount to anything.

Around this same time, the unions at American and US Airways made their presence felt on the lobbying front. One union leader in particular, Laura Glading, then president of the APFA, was front and center in that effort. Glading, a 35-year employee of American, was motivated by one thing—she desperately wanted this merger to be approved. Like a dog on a bone, Glading had pushed the same agenda tirelessly practically from the day American filed for bankruptcy.

The unions organized a September 18 rally in Washington, D.C., in support of the merger. Several hundred employees of both companies, many flying on company aircraft chartered for the occasion, descended on the nation's capital. Following the rally, the employees broke into small groups and walked the halls of Congress, dropping in on dozens of senators and representatives to garner support for the merger.

Union leaders went one step further. They arranged for a private meeting with Bill Baer and members of his staff. For a government agency that's allegedly immune from outside influence, it was a feather in the cap of union leaders that Baer agreed to meet with them, particularly with a trial set to begin two months later.

Several days after the employee rally in Washington, Bruce Wark and I continued our discussions with Abbott's chief of staff. Daniel Hodge was cordial and professional throughout the negotiations. It was evident that he had the ear of Attorney General Abbott, and we formulated the outline of a deal in record time. Likewise, when it came down to resolving open issues, Abbott was easy to work with. I can't take much credit for the deal because the state was so anxious to get out of the litigation.

The settlement with Texas was announced at a news conference at the Admirals Club in DFW's Terminal D on October 1. The terms of the agreement were simple. We agreed to a number of "behavioral" remedies, the kind of remedies that Justice had no interest in.

We promised to keep our headquarters in the DFW area, to maintain DFW Airport as a major hub, and to retain daily service to the twenty-two Texas cities we currently served, for at least three years. In other words, the settlement required us to do exactly what we were planning to do all along.

With the State of Texas out of the lawsuit, the litigation team began discussions with other state attorneys general to see if they would settle along similar terms. I was well aware, and the US Airways team was quick to remind me, that a settlement with Texas and other states was not worth much in the long run. DOJ was the big problem and it didn't appear that they had much enthusiasm for settlement.

The trial clock continued to advance its march to November 25. Depositions were in full swing, expert witnesses endeavored to put final touches on econometric reports, and the trial team worked on trial briefs and exhibits. As the date of the trial drew near, any chance of settling the case would require swift, decisive action.

We worked hard with US Airways to craft an offer of settlement, but it proved difficult to assemble a package that everyone could live with. We hated the idea of parting with assets that other airlines would acquire and use to compete against us. But we had little choice if we were serious about settling the lawsuit. The package we finally agreed to included valuable gates and slots at key airports, including Washington Reagan and LaGuardia. We hoped the proposed divestiture would ameliorate part of DOJ's concern that the newly merged entity would control a disproportionate amount of scarce airport resources. I was anxious to hear what DOJ thought of our offer.

DOJ officials, primarily Baer and Hesse, told us they found our proposal intriguing and liked a good portion of it, but claimed it did not go far enough. They then teed up a strange negotiating tactic, one that I had never before encountered. The tactic was the brainchild of Bill Baer.

Hesse delivered Baer's message. He insisted that we place all of American's DCA slot holdings on the table as the entrée to further settlement negotiations. Analogizing it to a game of poker, the American slots were the "ante" to enter the game. At that time, American controlled 104 takeoff and landing slots, excluding slots held for commuter aircraft operations.

No one understood the logic behind Baer's negotiating stance. Why not just reject our original offer and make a counteroffer, one that included 104 DCA slots? It reminded me of a child refusing to share his toys until the other children gave him their toys first.

US Airways was adamant that we reject Baer's "ante up" maneuver and walk away from further settlement discussions. They worried that if we acquiesced to Baer's demand, he would take the 104 slots, put them in his back pocket, then make even greater demands. I understood why they took this position. A flat-out refusal to play Baer's game may have forced Baer to abandon his position, particularly if he was getting cold feet about the trial. It was impossible to know whether he was bluffing and, with trial staring us in the face, we didn't have time to find out.

I believed that we should accede to Baer's demand so we could learn the full extent of their counteroffer. I figured that Baer must have at least some modicum of interest in settlement or he would have rejected our offer out of hand. If we found the DOJ counter unreasonable, we could easily reject it and proceed to trial. No harm, no foul.

The question of whether to put the DCA slots on the table was a difficult one. Everyone, it seemed, had an opinion as we tried to make sense of what Baer and company had in mind. In the end, whether to accept Baer's slot perquisite was a decision for the two airlines, not outside counsel. American favored the slot ante and US Airways was reticent to put the slots into play. Back and forth we went. We appreciated that the ante was tantamount to highway robbery, and US Airways was mindful that a rejection of the ante might permanently close the door to settlement.

The issue was resolved when Horton called Parker during the weekend of October 26 to press the case. Parker told Horton that he needed to speak with his board. In the meantime, I told Jack Butler that American was pushing to accept Baer's crazy settlement overture. Surely Butler could no longer assert that American was looking for ways to scuttle the merger.

Parker received clearance from his board, and on Monday outside counsel called Renata Hesse and gave her the news—the two airlines were prepared to put American's 104 DCA slots on the negotiating table in exchange for the privilege of learning what lay behind the settlement curtain. The next day, Tuesday, October 29, DOJ delivered on its promise and gave us the counteroffer. In addition to the one hundred and four slots at Washington Reagan, the DOJ demanded thirty-four slots at LaGuardia, and two gates each at Boston, Chicago, Los Angeles, Miami, and Dallas Love Field airports. We also had to relinquish an adequate number of gates and support facilities needed to operate the gates and slots at these airports.

And there it was. The minimum ante to play Baer's version of Texas Hold'em was steep, but the rest of the cards in his hand amounted to a pair of deuces. Baer's counteroffer was not the draconian asset divestiture we feared. Sure, it would be painful to disgorge these assets, particularly those at Washington Reagan and LaGuardia, but it could have been much worse. It was clear that the DOJ wanted to avoid trial. Otherwise, the "ask" would have been much larger. The exaggerated harm to the consumer alleged in Baer's complaint would not be remedied by this settlement.

Both airlines groused about DOJ's offer of settlement, particularly the assets at DCA and LaGuardia. US Airways was also unhappy about the Love Field divestiture, but I likened those gates to a "briar patch." We tried on multiple occasions over the years to carve a niche at Love Field, but it never worked. With our large hub at DFW and Southwest's overwhelming presence at Love Field, I wasn't particularly troubled by the proposed divestiture of those gates. Chicago, Los Angeles, and Boston gates and facilities were all valuable assets, but a rounding error in the big scheme of things. Besides, while not yet addressed, we would push to sell the asset package to other carriers and recapture at least a portion of the lost value.

Despite our displeasure with the asset divestiture, American and US Airways agreed that we should accept DOJ's counteroffer. First, we needed approval from our respective boards of directors.

On the American side, we set a telephonic meeting with our board for Thursday, October 31. Horton opened the meeting and gave a brief overview of the events of the previous few days. He then asked me to describe the details of the DOJ's offer of settlement.

I laid out the specifics of the deal, including a reminder that we had yet to reach agreement with the remaining six plaintiff states and the District of Columbia. I told them those discussions were far advanced and would not likely pose a problem. When I finished speaking, the board asked several questions, but it was evident they were in favor of the deal. They quickly gave us the green light to move forward. My long ago promise to the board that regulatory approval would be a "walk in the park" proved inaccurate, but I was pleased that we were now close to the finish line.

Like American, Doug Parker and his team assembled their board to discuss the proposed settlement. We soon received word that the US Airways board had given its nod of approval.

Even with the basic outline of the deal agreed to, drafting and negotiating a settlement agreement of this size is a time-consuming and frustrating task. Nevertheless, we plowed headlong into the process. We encountered a number of stumbling blocks, but none large enough to derail the course of settlement. For example, while the settlement agreement required us to divest two gates at each of seven airports, reaching a consensus as to the location of those gates and the ancillary operational facilities associated with the gates (like baggage delivery space and ramp ready rooms) was not easy.

Another difficult issue concerned the process under which American and US Airways would dispose of the slots and gates. We needed an understanding about how other airlines would go about purchasing the assets and at what price. We also needed agreement concerning the process that would be followed if more than one airline expressed an interest in the gates and slots, and what would happen if no airline wanted the assets.

As we worked through the details of the settlement, negotiations with the six remaining plaintiff states and the District of Columbia took on a more urgent tone. In a strange twist, the states demanded behavioral remedies that exceeded those we agreed to with the

State of Texas, including a broader commitment on the continued operation of major hubs and a five-year term instead of three years. We pushed back, believing that Justice would stay out of the fray. Instead, the DOJ locked arms with the states, informing us that they would not settle unless we reached a satisfactory resolution with all plaintiffs. We knew the states were in no position to try the lawsuit on their own, so DOJ's solidarity with the states served only to further embolden their cause. It was a classic case of the gnat firmly planting itself on the rear end of the horse for a free ride.

After much haggling, we finally reached an accommodation with the plaintiff states. We agreed to continue to operate hubs in Philadelphia, Charlotte, Miami, Chicago, Phoenix, Los Angeles, and JFK (in addition to the existing DFW hub commitment) for a period of three years. We also agreed to operate daily service for five years to 46 cities spread among the six plaintiff states (later amending from three to five years the service commitment we made to the State of Texas).

With the state settlements behind us, we swiftly wrapped up loose ends with the DOJ. It was difficult to believe that the deal was complete. Against terrible odds, the parties found a way to thread the needle and reach an agreement that avoided the risk and uncertainties of a trial. A formal announcement of the settlement was made on November 12, 2013.

The DOJ declared the settlement a victory on behalf of consumers. "This agreement has the potential to shift the landscape of the airline industry. By guaranteeing a bigger foothold for low-cost carriers at key U.S. airports, this settlement ensures airlines passengers will see more competition on nonstop and connecting routes throughout the country," United States Attorney General Eric Holder said in a statement. Bill Baer went further, claiming the settlement would "disrupt the cozy relationships among the incumbent legacy carriers, increase access to key congested airports and provide consumers with more choices and more competitive airfares on flights all across the country."

Tom Horton heralded the deal as an important day "for our customers, our people and our financial stakeholders" and Parker thanked employees who "voiced their support passionately and consistently" and elected officials, business leaders, and customers who "endorsed and supported this effort." The marketplace voiced its support of the deal by driving up AMR's stock price by 27 percent on the day of the announcement.

Commentators lined up on both sides of the aisle. Many considered the settlement a great result for consumers and the airline industry, while others questioned whether the DOJ acquiesced to political pressure, citing the intense lobbying effort undertaken by the two carriers.

From my perspective, the chatter was academic. It didn't really matter to me whether people liked or disliked the deal. Either way, the announcement paved the way for final bankruptcy clearance from Judge Lane. We received that clearance at a hearing on November 27, the day before Thanksgiving. Everything was now in place—we set the official closing of the merger for Monday morning, December 9, 2013.

The morning of the closing was a bitterly cold day in Dallas-Fort Worth. The temperature barely climbed above freezing, and ice still covered many freeway overpasses from a storm the week before. At approximately 6 a.m., I parked my car and took an elevator to the third floor of Weil, Gotshal & Manges's Dallas office. I walked into a conference room overlooking the Dallas skyline.

I sat down at the conference table and made small talk with a few of the roughly two dozen people present. There was a speakerphone in the middle of the table. David Gail, the young, yet accomplished, Weil Gotshal associate, was busy attending to last-minute details. There were approximately seventy-five participants on the conference call, all waiting patiently for the 6:20 a.m. call to begin.

Everyone in the room and those participating by phone were assembled for one purpose. This morning, the merger between American Airlines and US Airways would officially be finished. The official completion, or closing as it is called, was a carefully scripted affair and, in reality, quite a dull event.

I had only one task that morning, as did Steve Johnson from US Airways. When it came time, David Gail asked me to respond to a single compound question: "Have all closing conditions been satisfied and do you release your signature pages?" My response was a simple one-word answer: "Yes." Gail then asked Steve Johnson the same question. His reply was identical to mine. Within twenty minutes, it was all over. AMR Corporation, parent of American Airlines, and US Airways Group, parent of US Airways, became a single corporate entity known as the American Airlines Group.

As the participants on the phone hung up, the conference doors swung open and, despite the early hour, bottles of Veuve Clicquot champagne were uncorked for a quick congratulatory toast. I didn't stick around for more than a few minutes. I thanked those present and headed out.

Where should I go? I thought about driving to the American headquarters building where the new executives were gathering before a cheering crowd to celebrate the closing and usher in the next chapter in the company's history. But, my journey as general counsel, one that began on January 27, 2003, was now complete.

In my mind, I had said goodbye to American the previous day. I had driven with my wife, Michele, and my youngest daughter, Isabel, to the American Airlines headquarters. We parked in the visitor lot in front of the building and walked in. Michele and Isabel headed to the elevators, but I decided to take one final walk up the five flights of stairs to my office.

For the second time in twenty-nine years, I violated American's rules of conduct. I sat at my desk and pulled a bottle of wine from my briefcase. I placed it, along with a handwritten note addressed to Elise Eberwein, on my desk. Doug Parker selected Elise as the new executive vice president of people and communications, and she would occupy my office in the days following my departure. In my note to Elise, I told her it had been a privilege to sit in that office for so many years, and I wished her well.

Isabel immediately began to rifle through the desk drawers, looking for candy or mints, just as she had done many times over the previous ten years. To her disappointment, there wasn't much to find. When she came across a pair of scissors and stapler, she asked if we could take them home. I told her I thought we should leave them in the desk.

We left the office, walked through the halls, and past the Executive Committee meeting room where so many battles were fought, and so many decisions made, some better than others. It was a bittersweet moment. We left the executive wing and walked in the direction of the elevators. I paused, considered taking the stairs, but decided it was time for a change. We took the elevator to the ground floor, where I walked out of the American Airlines headquarters for the last time.

EPILOGUE

In the years following my departure from American, I've had lots of time to reflect on the events that shaped the company, particularly the bankruptcy and merger with US Airways. One thing that struck me is the enormous respect and appreciation I have for the lawyers and other professionals who represented the company, particularly during times of extraordinary challenge. While the cost of the professional and legal fees eclipsed 300 million dollars, I gained enormous respect for the men and women who devoted their time and talents to advance the company's agenda. The services provided and the results obtained were remarkable. I owe them a great debt of gratitude.

American Airlines filed for bankruptcy on November 29, 2011. The very nature of a bankruptcy proceeding carries great risk to the debtor and its constituencies. Typically, creditors, shareholders, and employees suffer significant adverse economic consequences. However, the American bankruptcy was anything but typical. In our case, all creditors were paid in full, the vast majority of employees kept their jobs and received pay increases, and existing shareholders recovered billions of dollars. In fact, the total value received by AMR shareholders exceeded 10 billion dollars. While American's bankruptcy was fraught with uncertainty, the final outcome was astonishing. It was one of the most successful corporate restructurings ever recorded.

Historically, the U.S. airline industry has been a fragile enterprise, beset by extraordinary financial losses and large numbers of airline failures and bankruptcies. Today, the industry seems to have shaken the financial malaise and is poised for a brighter future. In the four years since the closing, American Airlines has prospered, along with the rest of the airline industry. Buoyed by dramatically lower fuel prices, strong passenger demand, and only modest capacity increases, the industry is enjoying record profits. In 2016, American made a pretax profit of 4.3 billion dollars and the ten largest U.S. publicly traded commercial airlines recorded a total pretax profit of twenty-two billion dollars, a 14 percent margin.

The central issue is whether airline consolidation has materially altered the fundamentals of the industry. Is the industry now able to weather downturns in the economy, or substantial increases in the price of fuel, or external events like terrorist attacks? I don't know the answer to these questions, but I believe the industry is much better positioned than it has been over the last forty years to withstand these kinds of events. And, if that is true, airline passengers, employees, and shareholders will all benefit from a healthier industry.

Consistent with a statement I made during the Congressional hearings concerning the AA/US Airways merger, a strong United States airline industry is a matter of vital importance to this country. U.S. airlines transport in excess of eight hundred million passengers across our country and around the world every year, along with millions of tons of freight and mail. Collectively, airlines contribute billions of dollars to the U.S. economy.

Most importantly, the U.S. airline safety record is exemplary. Airlines routinely pack hundreds of passengers and luggage into a long, narrow tube that hurtles down a runway at over 100 miles an hour, ascends to an altitude of 35,000 feet, then rockets across the countryside at speeds exceeding 500 miles an hour, all while passengers enjoy a meal, a movie, or surf the internet.

At the conclusion of the journey, the aircraft gently lands and passengers disembark, with scarcely a moment of thought given to the miracle of flight. This same routine occurs nearly twenty-seven thousand times every day of the year. And, the airline safety record is extraordinary. In the ten years ending December 31, 2016, only forty-seven passengers died on commercial U.S. airlines. By comparison, more than 350,000 people were killed in automobile accidents during that same time period.

The astonishing airline safety record is attributable to a host of factors, including the remarkable technology developed by aircraft and jet engine manufacturers, along with the important contributions of the Department of Transportation and the Federal Aviation Administration. But I attribute most of the credit to the dedicated employees of American Airlines and the employees of other commercial airlines. Every day, pilots, flight attendants, mechanics, flight dispatch and control tower personnel, airport agents, meteorologists, baggage handlers, and a long list of others, perform their duties with meticulous precision to ensure the safety of all passengers who board U. S. commercial aircraft.

The traveling public experiences firsthand the work performed by the pilots and flight attendants of American Airlines. They are among the very best in the world. But many equally important American employees go entirely unnoticed by most passengers. Have you ever wondered who calculates how much fuel is needed for each flight, or the proper weight and balance of each aircraft? Or what about the man or woman crouching deep inside the belly of an aircraft who ensures that luggage and cargo are properly loaded? Or the mechanic who repairs a nonfunctioning electrical circuit shortly before departure? These invisible workers are all part of the carefully choreographed ballet of flight that occurs each and every day. It's no great surprise that the Air Transport World named American Airlines the 2017 Airline of the Year.

Following my retirement, I have remained in close contact with several of the people who played a significant role in the events described in these pages. Others, I have not.

After his departure from American Airlines, Don Carty served in a variety of business capacities, including vice chairman and CFO of Dell, chairman of Virgin America, chairman of Porter Airlines, and the board of directors of Hawaiian Airlines, CN Rail, Talisman

Energy, EMC and others. I remain thankful to Don for appointing me general counsel of American in 2003.

Gerard Arpey serves on three corporate boards. He is vice chairman of SC Johnson, and a member of the board of Home Depot and American Beacon, an asset management company. He is also an advisor to Emerald Creek Group, a private equity company located in California. When not attending board meetings, he spends as much time as possible flying private aircraft and fly fishing.

Like Arpey, Tom Horton loves to fly private aircraft and is an avid fly fisherman. Horton is the lead director of Qualcomm and serves on the board of Walmart. In October 2015, Horton joined private equity firm Warburg Pincus as a senior advisor.

Doug Parker continues in his role as chairman and CEO of American Airlines. While I never had the opportunity to work directly with him, it appears that he is doing an outstanding job leading the airline.

Following the merger, Scott Kirby served as president of American Airlines until he became the odd man out in an August 2016 management shake-up. The board promoted chief operating officer Robert Isom to president and Scott Kirby then joined United Airlines as its president.

Steve Johnson is an executive vice president at American with a wide-ranging set of responsibilities, including legal, government and regulatory matters, labor relations, real estate, and airport affairs. He continues to be a close confidant and advisor to Doug Parker.

Bev Goulet was one of the few AA senior executives who remained at the company following the merger. As executive vice president and chief integration officer, she was responsible for integrating the operations of the two airlines. Goulet retired from the company in June 2017. She now serves on the boards of Rolls-Royce and Xenia Hotels & Resorts. I miss working alongside my former colleague.

Tom Roberts retired from Weil Gotshal in 2016. He remains involved in a variety of business pursuits, including service as the lead director and audit committee chair of MGM Growth Properties, a publicly traded REIT. He and his wife spend most of their time at their home on Kiawah Island, South Carolina, where they enjoy indulging their six grandchildren.

Steve Karotkin continues to handle large corporate bankruptcy cases at Weil Gotshal. Karotkin's sense of humor remains intact.

Karotkin's mentor and colleague, Harvey Miller, was diagnosed with ALS and died in April 2015 at the age of eighty-two.

Jack Butler retired as a partner at Skadden Arps in early 2014 and joined Hilco Global. Two years later, Jack founded Birch Lake Holdings, a company that provides a variety of financial restructuring and M&A services. I spoke with Jack in May 2017 and we talked about his new business and the success of the American bankruptcy. I wished him well.

ACKNOWLEDGMENTS

For two years after retiring from American Airlines, I toyed with the idea of writing this book. Struggling with the decision, I sought advice from Mark Curriden, the owner and publisher of *The Texas Lawbook* and an accomplished author.

I invited Mark to lunch to pitch my idea for the book. Mark had interviewed me several times when I was general counsel at American so I prepared myself for an onslaught of questions. Instead, Mark listened carefully as I outlined what I had in mind. When I finished, Mark's response was straightforward and emphatic: "Stop thinking and start writing." I realize that was the push I needed. Mark provided a steady stream of advice as the project moved forward. I appreciate his support.

Soon after meeting with Mark, I called Terry Maxon, a former aviation reporter for *The Dallas Morning News*. When I asked if he wanted to collaborate on the book, he said yes without hesitation. Terry provided a virtual treasure chest of information drawn from his airline blog and his twenty-five years as an aviation reporter. His expertise in aviation history and his eye for detail kept us on path throughout the long days and months devoted to this project. This book would not have been possible without Terry's involvement.

As I put pen to paper, I turned to my wife, Michele Valdez, for much needed assistance. As an attorney and former employee of American Airlines, she was familiar with many of the issues and the people involved. I questioned Michele endlessly—at dinner, on vacation, while playing tennis—about the best way to present topics covered in the book. We often debated issues long into the night. But her greatest contribution was the long hours she devoted to editing each chapter and her additions of much needed color commentary. She pushed me to be a better writer and I am incredibly thankful for her patience and advice.

As each chapter was completed, I sent them to my mother, Arlene Kennedy. She is an avid reader and provided great feedback. I appreciate the encouragement she gave as the project moved forward.

From our first meeting, Nena Oshman and Austin Miller of the Dupree Miller & Associates literary agency had confidence in our ability to tell this story. Thank you for sticking with us and for introducing us to Savio Republic, our publisher. As experts in the world of publishing, they endured our many questions and guided us every step of the way. And thank you all for bringing this project to fruition.

I am indebted to many of my former colleagues at the company. To the CEOs of American Airlines who served during and after the years covered by this book—Don Carty, Gerard Arpey, Tom Horton, and Doug Parker—thank you for reviewing the manuscript and for your willingness to share insights and stories that added greatly to the telling of this story. Thank you to Elise Eberwein, Bev Goulet, Ken Wimberly, Will Ris, and Jeff Brundage who reviewed excerpts of the manuscript and provided valuable input and additions to the book.

Thank you to the University of Utah S. J. Quinney College of Law for providing a first-rate legal education and the essential tools needed to navigate complex legal issues as general counsel of a major corporation. For this, I am deeply indebted.

There are a great number of other people, both inside and outside the company, whose assistance was essential to the telling of this story. I am particularly grateful to Chris Christensen at Condon & Forsyth.

When the book was complete, I engaged Mike Powell, a senior partner at Locke Lord in Dallas, to review the manuscript from a legal perspective. I appreciate his careful reading of the manuscript, and for the insights and suggestions he provided.

As Terry and I wrote this book, we did our best to ensure that it accurately reflects the events depicted and is factually correct. We recognize there may be a few mistakes and for that we apologize.

Gary Kennedy

BIBLIOGRAPHY

CHAPTER 2

Form 10-K for FYs 1993-2000, AMR Corp., various dates of filing.

"The Business-Cycle Peak of March 2001," National Bureau of Economic Research, November 26, 2001.

"AMR on a heading for bankruptcy," Eric Torbenson, *The Dallas Morning News*, January 23, 2003.

"Integrated United States Security Database (IUSSD): Data on the Terrorist Attacks in the United States Homeland, 1970 to 2011," National Consortium for the Study of Terrorism and Responses to Terrorism, December 2012.

"The 9/11 Commission Report," Final Report of the National Commission on Terrorist Attacks Upon the United States, July 22, 2004.

"Statement of Gerard P. Arpey to the National Commission on Terrorist Attacks Upon The United States," January 27, 2004, Seventh public hearing, the National Commission on Terrorist Attacks Upon the United States.

CHAPTER 3

Form 10-K for FY 2002, AMR Corp., filed April 15, 2003.

"AMR announces new leadership," news release, American Airlines, April 24, 2003.

CHAPTER 4

"American Airlines charts course for brighter future, CEO Arpey Unveils Turnaround Plan at Annual Meeting," news release, American Airlines, May 21, 2003.

Form 10-K for FY 2003, AMR Corp., filed February 27, 2004.

"AMR directors hit by fallout," Andrew Countryman, Chicago Tribune, April 27, 2003.

CHAPTER 5

"American Struggles with Costs, Unions as Mergers Boost Rivals," Mary Schlangenstein, Bloomberg News, September 21, 2010.

"American Airlines pilots protest manager stock bonuses," Trebor Banstetter and David Wethe, *Fort Worth Star-Telegram*, April 18, 2007.

CHAPTER 7

"The Crash of Flight 587: Belle Harbor; 5 Neighbors Gone, and a Jet Engine Where a Child's Bike Might Have Been," Dan Barry And Elissa Gootman, *The New York Times*, November 14, 2001.

"Who They Were / The Victims of American Flight 587," Karen Freifeld as lead reporter, *Newsday*, November 27, 2001.

"In-Flight Separation of Vertical Stabilizer, American Airlines Flight 587, Airbus Industrie A300-605R, N14053, Belle Harbor, New York, November 12, 2001," National Transportation Safety Board report adopted October 26, 2004.

CHAPTER 8

Form 10-K for fiscal year 2000, AMR Corp., filed March 22, 2001.

Form 10-K for fiscal year 2008, AMR Corp., filed February 19, 2009.

"American Airlines parent AMR raises $2.9B, adds flights in Dallas, other major hubs," Terry Maxon, *The Dallas Morning News*, September 17, 2009.

"United Airlines Takes Aim at Rival Carrier," Trevor Jensen, *Adweek*, March 17, 2005.

CHAPTER 9

"American Airlines appeals directly to its pilots with latest contract offer," Terry Maxon Airline Biz blog, *The Dallas Morning News*, November 14, 2011.

"APA board votes 17-1 to send letter to AMR chairman and CEO Gerard Arpey," Terry Maxon, Airline Biz blog, *The Dallas Morning News*, November 15, 2011.

CHAPTER 10

"AMR to File Chapter 11 Today," Terry Maxon, *The Dallas Morning News*, November 29, 2011.

"AMR and American Airlines File for Chapter 11 Reorganization to Achieve Industry Competitiveness," news release, American Airlines, November 29, 2011.

"A C.E.O.'s Moral Stand," D. Michael Lindsay, *The New York Times*, November 30, 2011.

Transcript of court hearing, U.S. Bankruptcy Judge Sean Lane, November 29, 2011.

CHAPTER 11

"PBGC Director Josh Gotbaum on the Importance of American Airlines' Pension Plans," news release, Pension Benefit Guaranty Corporation, January 12, 2012.

"American Airlines chief warns of looming cuts in employees, airplanes," Terry Maxon, *The Dallas Morning News*, December 15, 2011.

"Horton doesn't sound worried about a US Airways bid," Terry Maxon, Airline Biz blog, *The Dallas Morning News*, February 2, 2012.

"AMR plans to slash 13,000 jobs," Terry Maxon, Airline Biz blog, *The Dallas Morning News*, February 1, 2012.

"AMR CEO Tom Horton Sends Letter to American Airlines Employees," news release, American Airlines, February 1, 2012.

"Horton answers questions about American Airlines' restructuring plan," Terry Maxon, Airline Biz blog, *The Dallas Morning News*, February 1, 2012.

Transcript of court hearing, U.S. Bankruptcy Judge Sean Lane, March 22, 2012.

"American Airlines to ask bankruptcy judge to toss out labor contracts," Terry Maxon, Airline Biz blog, *The Dallas Morning News*, March 22, 2012.

CHAPTER 12

"Rivals Eye American Airlines; Delta, US Airways Among Potential Buyers as Wave of Consolidation Continues," Gina Chon, Susan Carey and Mike Spector, *The Wall Street Journal*, January 13, 2012.

"Horton doesn't sound worried about a US Airways bid," Terry Maxon, Airline Biz blog, *The Dallas Morning News*, February 2, 2012.

CHAPTER 13

"Memorandum of Decision, Re: Debtor's Motion To Reject Collective Bargaining Agreements Pursuant To 11 U.S.C. Section 1113 As It Relates To The Allied Pilots Association," U.S. Bankruptcy Judge Sean Lane, August 15, 2012.

"APA defends the need for maintenance write-ups," Terry Maxon, Airline Biz blog, *The Dallas Morning News*, September 28, 2012.

"Order of Contempt," U.S. District Judge Joe Kendall, U.S. District Court for the Northern District of Texas, February 13, 1999.

CHAPTER 14

"US Airways execs: American Airlines merger would bring $1.2 billion-plus in benefits," Terry Maxon, *The Dallas Morning News*, April 25, 2012.

CHAPTER 17

U.S. Department of Justice lawsuit versus American Airlines and Robert L. Crandall, U.S. District Court for the Northern District of Texas, February 22, 1983.

"American Airlines Target of U.S. Suit," Robert D. Hershey Jr., *The New York Times*, February 24, 1983.

CHAPTER 18

"Justice official: Here's why we're fighting the US Airways-American Airlines merger," Terrey Maxon, Airline Biz blog, *The Dallas Morning News*, August 13, 2013.

"Greg Abbott shares views with local Republicans," Jennifer Rios, (San Angelo, Texas) *Standard-Times*, February 13, 2013.

Transcript of court hearing, U.S. Bankruptcy Judge Sean Lane, August 15, 2013.

"American Airlines has no Plan B, will take antitrust fight to court," Mark Curriden, *The Dallas Morning News*, August 20, 2013.

CHAPTER 19

"Justice Department Requires US Airways and American Airlines to Divest Facilities at Seven Key Airports to Enhance System-wide Competition and Settle Merger Challenge," news release, US. Department of Justice, November 12, 2013.

"Assistant Attorney General Bill Baer Delivers Remarks at the Conference Call Regarding the Justice Department's Proposed Settlement with US Airways and American Airlines," news release, U.S. Department of Justice, November 12, 2013.

"AMR Corporation and US Airways Announce Settlement with U.S. Department of Justice and State Attorneys General," joint news release, American Airlines and US Airways, November 12, 2013.

EPILOGUE

Form 10-K annual report, 2016, American Airlines Group.

"Corrected 2016 Traffic Data for U.S Airlines and Foreign Airlines U.S. Flights," news release, Bureau of Transportation Statistics, March 27, 2017.

"2016 Annual and 4th Quarter Airline Financial Data," news release, Bureau of Transportation Statistics, May 2, 2017.

"Accidents Involving Passenger Fatalities: U. S. Airlines (Part 121) 1982–Present," National Transportation Safety Board.

Highway fatality numbers, Insurance Institute for Highway Safety and National Safety Council